What people are saying about …

SPEAK LIFE

"This book is a must-read for anyone who is serious about their relationship with God and their ability to speak life into relationships. Our words are powerful, and Brady Boyd gives us great wisdom in this very timely book. Thank you, Pastor Brady, for writing something that will help all of us follow Jesus better!"

Tommy Barnett, co-pastor and founder of
Dream City Church in Arizona and founder
of the Dream Center in Los Angeles

"Our words have so much power—both to hurt others and to build them up. In *Speak Life*, Brady Boyd reminds us that our first conversation before opening our mouths must be a silent one with God. When we follow Christ's example and keep in constant communication with our Father, we are then equipped to face every situation with his divine power, wisdom, and grace. *Speak Life* will forever change the way you think about the words you pray and the words you say."

Chris Hodges, senior pastor of
Church of the Highlands and author
of *Fresh Air* and *Four Cups*

"Brady Boyd has done it again. In *Speak Life*, Boyd writes about something that every one of us can understand on many levels: the power of words and conversations. Boyd writes from a pastor's heart. And by this, I'm not suggesting that he writes as a guru, an expert, or a know-it-all. Rather, he shares with raw honesty and vulnerability; but through it all, he faithfully points people to Jesus, the Scriptures, and ultimately, to a more intimate relationship with God."

Rev. Eugene Cho, senior pastor of Quest
Church and author of *Overrated*

"Have you ever said something you wanted to take back? At some point, we've all been careless with our words. But the truth is, the quality of life we live depends on what we say. In Brady Boyd's new book, *Speak Life*, he addresses this topic with clear and practical biblical answers. I know you'll be challenged and inspired as you learn to speak words that bring life."

Robert Morris, founding senior pastor
of Gateway Church and bestselling
author of *The Blessed Life*, *The Power
of Your Words*, and *Truly Free*

"Brady Boyd brilliantly excavates Jesus's conversational style. Discover how to look, sound, and act more like Jesus as *Speak Life* positions you to 'speak life' into any situation. Your communication habits will be radically transformed."

John and Lisa Bevere, founders
of Messenger International

"Brady Boyd has written another really helpful, down-to-earth book. Open to any page and you'll find practical wisdom that speaks straight to where you are."

John Eldredge, author of *Wild at Heart* and *Moving Mountain*

"I absolutely love this book! God has given Brady Boyd incredible revelation about the power of words and how they should be used to build and enhance every relationship in our lives—including the way we relate to God and ourselves. This book is a must-read for everyone! It will truly change your life and increase your potential for success on every level."

Jimmy Evans, founder and CEO of MarriageToday

"We all know the power of the right word spoken at the right time. Words like that can turn a bad day around or even change a life. When it comes to speaking the right words at the right time, no one did it better than Jesus. What if we learned to speak like him—to have the sorts of conversations that helped people meet with God? That's what *Speak Life* is all about. I'm excited for my friend Brady's new book because, in my experience, we could all stand to sound a little bit more like Jesus!"

Greg Surratt, senior pastor of Seacoast Church

"The wonderful gifts we draw from *Speak Life* are wisdom and experience for developing excellent relationships. Of course, the Word of God is the foundation of this valuable work, which is a genuine treasure for those of us wishing to develop a wholesome communication with our heavenly Father and those around us. Thank you, Brady, for helping us rediscover the power of our words!"

Pastor Cash Luna, senior pastor of
Casa de Dios in Guatemala City

"Speak Life is a fantastic weapon to put in your artillery against the Enemy. It will equip you to go to new levels in your spiritual walk and give you tools for advancing the kingdom of God. A must-read!"

Christine Caine, Founder of A21 and
Propel Women, author of *Unashamed*

"Brady Boyd 'nailed it' in *Speak Life*. After reading this book, my understanding of some personal choices I need to make smacked me right between the eyes. The insights you will discover about the crucial conversations in your life will make you a stronger believer, a better person, and a more effective leader. Put this book on your 'to read now' list, and buy a copy for the people you love the most."

Philip Wagner, pastor of Oasis Church in
Los Angeles, founder of Generosity.org, and
author of *Love Works* and *Unlock Your Dream*

SPEAK LIFE

SPEAK LIFE

RESTORING HEALTHY COMMUNICATION
IN HOW YOU THINK, TALK, AND PRAY

BRADY BOYD

David C Cook®
transforming lives together

SPEAK LIFE
Published by David C Cook
4050 Lee Vance View
Colorado Springs, CO 80918 U.S.A.

David C Cook U.K., Kingsway Communications
Eastbourne, East Sussex BN23 6NT, England

The graphic circle C logo is a registered trademark of David C Cook.

All rights reserved. Except for brief excerpts for review purposes,
no part of this book may be reproduced or used in any form
without written permission from the publisher.

The website addresses recommended throughout this book are offered as a resource
to you. These websites are not intended in any way to be or imply an endorsement
on the part of David C Cook, nor do we vouch for their content.

Details in some stories have been changed to protect the identities of the persons involved.

The author has added italics to Scripture quotations for emphasis.

LCCN 2016939759
ISBN 978-1-4347-0689-8
eISBN 978-1-4347-1093-2

The Author is represented by the literary agency of Alive Communications, Inc., 7680
Goddard Street, Suite 200, Colorado Springs, CO 80920. www.alivecommunications.com.

The Team: Kyle Duncan, Amy Konyndyk, Jennifer Lonas,
Helen Macdonald, Abby DeBenedittis, Susan Murdock
Cover Design: Nick Lee
Cover Photo: Shutterstock

Printed in the United States of America
First Edition 2016

1 2 3 4 5 6 7 8 9 10

For my parents, Leland and Pat. You told me I would be okay, and I believed you despite overwhelming evidence to the contrary. You spoke life to me, and for that I am grateful.

CONTENTS

INTRODUCTION
THE FOUR CONVERSATIONS

My sixteen-year-old son, Abram, has been wrestling with some weighty relational issues lately, and several nights ago I noticed he was quieter than his typically chatty self. I asked what was up, but he wouldn't crack.

"I'm okay" was all he said, even though I knew that wasn't the truth.

So I left the room for a few minutes to have a quick chat with God. *I know something's wrong,* I told God.

In my spirit I sensed a divine yes.

What is it? I asked. *What's going on in my son's heart?*

In the space of a few seconds, God revealed to me the crux of Abram's problems: they had to do with a few relationships that had gotten sideways. Then God assured me that he would equip me to help Abram come out of his funk.

It's hard to describe what that felt like, and what a relief it was that I wasn't all alone in this situation with my son. When you're the parent of teenagers, it's tempting to want to check out from time to time, to take their words (or grunts, as the case may be) at face value, to put too much weight on the fact that you've raised them right and can just release them to the world. Things often work themselves out, after all.

The Enemy is forever whispering to parents of teens, *Let it go. It's just a phase. This will pass fast enough*, when in actuality, our teens need just as much attention and guidance—if not more—as they did when they were curious little toddlers prone to sticking their fingers into electrical sockets. Checking in with God that night reaffirmed my commitment to my son. Regardless of Satan's taunts to just leave Abram alone, I decided to wade into what could be a difficult conversation in the hope of helping my son sharpen his relational skills.

As I headed back into the room where Abram was hanging out, I felt a deep sense of inner confidence and peace in knowing my mission as my kids' dad. I knew what God had revealed to me, and I knew that I was the only person in Abram's life who had the relational, emotional, and spiritual currency with him to do what I was about to do.

"Abram," I said as I approached him, "if I can tell you exactly what's bugging you, will you agree to talk about it with me?"

He looked at me as if I'd lost my mind and decided to trot out my best street-magic impersonation right there, right then with him. But he couldn't resist the challenge. "Yes," he said plainly. "I will."

I sat down across from my son and proceeded to lay out three big situations that were driving him nuts, relational knots I knew he had no clue how to untie. I threw them out there boldly, numbering them on my fingers as I went, and once I'd said my piece, Abram looked at me with wide eyes and said,

"Dad—*for real*—how do you know all that? You were gone, like, three minutes just now."

What I told my son is what I want you to hear too: prophetic communication is not some party trick; it's simply following the progression Christ laid out for us, which involves *talking to God* before we choose to *open our mouths to communicate with others.*

When we operate with others as Christ did, we first hear from heaven. Then we work to keep our self-talk grounded. After that we stand firm against the schemes of the Enemy. And then— voilà!—we miraculously speak words of life. That's all I did with Abram that night, and that's all I'm asking of you.

In the pages that follow, I want to explain why we get ourselves into conversational trouble, as well as the most time-tested ways to get out of it. I want to explore Jesus's perfect example in hopes of adapting his practices for our (admittedly imperfect) lives. How often did he commune with the Father? Why didn't he fall into sin when he was tempted? How did he stay on mission every day? Why did his words carry such tremendous weight?

I want to provide a little encouragement that no matter how reckless you've been with your words over the course of your days— and no matter how much damage those words have done—you (*even you!*) can become someone who is known for speaking wise and healing words. Starting today you can steward every syllable. Starting now you can use every word for good.

A DIVINE CHANGE OF PLANS

Last summer I took a sabbatical from ministry—a weeks-long break that was rejuvenating and deep-down sweet. I was nearing the end of a stay at the beach with my family when I received a crystal-clear word from the Lord. I had been researching and drafting a brand-new book, but evidently, up in heaven, there had been a change of plans.

Table it, God said to my spirit. *I have another subject in mind.* From there I sensed divine prompting after divine prompting encouraging me to write on *words* instead—the power of words, the potential of words, and instructions for using words well.

I sat with the topic for several days, mulling over the possibilities. My wife, Pam, and I have two teenagers now, and we can't help but notice how much weight our words carry with them, both for good and for ill. Their words seem to matter more to us now too: with Abram, because they reveal the heart not of a child anymore but of a man unfolding right before our eyes; and with Callie, because she's always played it close to the vest—as she settles into adolescence, we're tuned in to every syllable the child chooses to speak.

My mind chased off to my congregation at New Life Church in Colorado Springs, where there were scores of examples of how words had affected different members. A grown man was struggling with self-concept issues because his father called him "idiot" when he was a boy. A single mom was left perplexed and heavy burdened on the heels of a relationship with a man who promised he loved her and that he'd always be around—and then suddenly wasn't. High schoolers wrestle with knowing what is true because the sheer volume of information—much of it errant—assaulting them each day is more than they can sort through.

Even in my own heart, I found wounds that words had left behind, stuff that happened decades ago that still haunts me today.

So I told God I was on board with the new direction, and thus this book on *words*—the hopes God has for them, the ways we steward them, and the impact they have on others.

THE MASTER COMMUNICATOR

As someone who says he knows and loves Jesus and who tries to look, sound, and act more like Jesus every day, I've read the Bible as part of my morning ritual for decades now. Once I knew I'd be working on a book about words, I began to notice in my reading that whenever Jesus interacted with another person, *not once* did he speak unwise words. His input was flawless. His words were always on the mark, his tone was always pitch perfect, and his emotions were always impeccably matched to the situation at hand. I wondered, *In seeking to be more like Jesus every day, is it possible for us to speak this way as well?*

I decided to head back to the beginning of Jesus's ministry to try to decode his conversational style, and what I discovered during this excavation changed everything for me.

Despite my intentions to plow through the Gospels one "Jesus interaction" at a time, I didn't get beyond the first month and a half of his earthly ministry before I was totally arrested by awe. A mere five or six weeks into his work, people who heard his teaching were "amazed." Luke 4:32 says that "his words had authority," a concept that immediately gave me pause for the simple fact that in more than two decades of pastoring, teaching, preaching, and leading, I have never known my words to *amaze* people. Sure, I've had a few popular sermons over the years, but Jesus's messages were immediately and unanimously amazing! I wanted to know more. What could possibly make a person's words so impactful? And could this wisdom somehow be imparted to an earthbound nondeity like me?

I scanned back a few verses in Luke 4 and saw the well-known words with fresh eyes. This is where Jesus entered the synagogue on the Sabbath and unrolled the scroll containing Isaiah's prophecy about the Messiah—about *him*. That day Jesus stood before his peers and read,

> The Spirit of the Lord is on me,
>> because he has anointed me
>> to proclaim good news to the poor.
> He has sent me to proclaim freedom for the
>> prisoners
>> and recovery of sight for the blind,
> to set the oppressed free,
>> to proclaim the year of the Lord's favor.
>> (vv. 18–19)

Jesus stood solidly on the ground of his mission—never wavering, never cowering, never ashamed. He knew who he was and operated confidently from that position. He was filled with God's Spirit, he was anointed for a purpose, and he was empowered to usher in freedom for those who found themselves enslaved.

Jesus's example convicted me. While I knew God called me for a specific reason—to leave radio broadcasting, to pastor a local church, to advocate for orphans and single moms and others who have been marginalized and scorned—I knew I didn't always operate from a place of certainty like Jesus. As proof, I had to acknowledge that during certain seasons of my life, my self-talk was made up almost completely of words of criticism and condemnation. Rarely did I offer myself acceptance, approval, or strength.

Rewinding even further in Luke 4, I saw that this expression of Jesus's confidence came right on the heels of the most intense season of testing he'd experienced as a man. The early verses detail the three temptations of Christ, when Satan tried to get him to put his God to the test. Jesus had been fasting and praying for forty straight days when this whole deal went down. You remember these temptations: first, there was the stone-to-bread challenge, which in my estimation was the cruelest of all—"Tell this stone to become bread" Satan taunted (v. 3). Essentially it was the equivalent of taking a gluten-free person to Panera Bread for lunch; the smell alone will do them in!

Second, there was the enticement to worship Satan in exchange for having power over every kingdom of the world, and third was the dare for Jesus to do a Peter Pan from the top of the temple, trusting God and his angels to break his fall.

In response to all three temptations, Jesus quoted Scripture back to the Enemy, citing his Father's words:

- "It takes more than bread to really live" (v. 4 THE MESSAGE).
- "Worship the Lord your God and only the Lord your God. Serve him with absolute single-heartedness" (v. 8 THE MESSAGE).
- "Don't you dare tempt the Lord your God" (v. 12 THE MESSAGE).

It was as if he were saying, "You come at me with temptations and taunts, Satan, but they don't stand a chance against truth."

I started putting these events together in my mind and could see that Jesus's ability to "amaze" people with words traced back to his certainty about his calling in life—"I'm the treasured dwelling place of the Holy Spirit, and I'm anointed to do some serious good." This calling was further reinforced as he stood firm against the Enemy's threats.

This was starting to get interesting. I felt as if I were cracking some secret conversational code.

Finally I scanned all the way back to the inception of Jesus's earthly ministry to find the starting point of the progression I would soon prize. Before Jesus spoke amazing words, before he showcased his sound self-talk, and even before he hit home runs off all three of Satan's trick pitches, there he was in conversation with his Father, worshipping his goodness, seeking his guidance, praying fervently, submitting to being baptized. In response "the sky opened up and the Holy Spirit, like a dove descending, came down on him. And along with the Spirit, a voice [from heaven said]: 'You are my Son, chosen and marked by my love, pride of my life'" (3:21–22 THE MESSAGE).

This is ultimately what was behind Jesus's ability to amaze people with his words; to deliver the right message at the right time, *every single time*; to practice self-restraint and amp up emotionally, depending on what the situation warranted; to speak words of light and life infused simultaneously with power and peace. Before he ever opened his mouth here on this earth, Jesus communed with his Father above. He refused to be reckless and brash with his words, choosing instead to be encouraging and wise. Jesus's use of words was, at its core, a *spiritual discipline.* I'd never seen communication in that light before.

WE *CAN* GET IT RIGHT

A friend stopped by the house last week on his way home from work and wanted to talk through some relational issues that were weighing him down. He detailed the dilemmas and then, tossing his hands in the air, said, "Brady, I just want to get it right."

"That's actually all any of us want," I responded.

While it often seems excruciatingly hard, the truth is, we *can* get it right. Specifically, we can stop wounding each other with our words, which is where every heartache really begins. We can learn to discern the voice of our heavenly Father, setting into motion a communications progression that sets us up to win.

We can finally tame our troublesome tongues, that "small rudder" on a huge ship that the apostle James said can set a useful course even in the face of the strongest winds (see James 3:3–4). We can become more like Jesus instead of settling for a lifetime of conversational regret. *We can move past the static of our lives and tune in with rapt attention to input from God.*

And so: this book.

I've arranged this book according to the four "conversations" Jesus had in the Luke 3–4 text we looked at earlier. In each part, I demonstrate the learning curve I've been on, offering stories that showcase the little victories I've experienced, as well as the myriad ways I've totally bungled my words. The net effect is a message that is simple and true: *you and I can get better at using our words to heal rather than to hurt.*

We can become more like Jesus in our communication, the One whose speech always brought life. We can learn to contemplate language instead of slinging selfish and foolish syllables. We can learn to live as modern-day prophets: people who hear from God first and then use words to strengthen, enlighten, and encourage. (Don't worry, you don't have to wear a robe or carry a staff to fit this bill.)

At the end of each chapter, you'll be invited to practice each of the four conversations in turn. Take advantage of these opportunities, and I think you'll start noticing that your heart will feel lighter, your words will come out wiser, and your relationships will become more life giving than they've ever been before. I'm rooting for you as you walk along wisdom's way, and God is rooting for you too. "If your heart is wise," he says, "then my heart will be glad indeed; my inmost being will rejoice" (Prov. 23:15–16).

THE FOUR CONVERSATIONS

God is eager to equip every one of us to use our words to bring not selfishness or haphazardness but rather encouragement and strength to life. This is a radical shift from how most people communicate. As it relates to the words we say to one another, we think the "thing" can be summed up in terms of extroversion or timing or winsomeness or quickness of wit, but there is so much more going on in our verbal exchanges. Every time I open my mouth to speak to you, I'm revealing how I've been doing in three other "conversations": what I'm saying to myself (self-talk), how well I'm refuting the lies of the Enemy, and how closely—if at all—I'm walking with God.

To the extent these three conversations—between me and God, between me and myself, and between me and Satan—are being managed poorly, I face a correspondingly higher risk of saying something idiotic and/or hurtful to the people I love. But to the extent these conversations are managed in the manner God intends, I will speak words that are relevant, authentic, life giving, and wise, and I will rarely—if ever—stick my foot in my mouth. I will be someone who *blesses*, not curses, with the words I speak in the fourth conversation: the one between you and me.

So how do we leverage the opportunity for good that exists each time we open our mouths to speak? One simple conversation will get that ball rolling, and it's the most important of the four: the one between you and God.

Conversation 1: Between You and God

Getting good at communicating well begins, interestingly enough, with prayer.

Prayer?

Yes. Right. *Prayer.*

It's important to steal away in the quiet of a given day to communicate with your heavenly Father, but equally important is the practice of speaking to him and hearing from him *while in conversation with others.* As words are flowing from your mouth, seek input in real time:

How can I serve your purposes in this person's life, God?
What words are fitting for this situation?
What are you after here, Lord?
Where are you working here?
How can I be of help?

When you and I seek God's wisdom—when we lean in to hear his voice and pursue divine insights before we open our mouths—we stand a 100 percent better chance of doing good instead of harm. Any conversation you have with another human being ought first to be a conversation between you and God: *What are you saying to me, Lord? What are you up to in my life? Why are you having me communicate with this person? And what do you want me to say?*

Conversation 2: Between You and Yourself

Come on, admit it. You talk to yourself too. The real question here is whether that self-talk is false or true.

Once you've checked in with God, it's wise to run some quick diagnostics on yourself. Is your self-talk helpful or harmful as you approach this exchange with someone else? Are you believing the best about God, about yourself, and about the person you're talking with? Or are you falling prey to lies?

This second conversation—the one that happens in your heart and head—is crucial. If your self-talk is laced with disparagement and denigration, then you're better off heading back to conversation number one and giving God an opportunity to recast that inner dialogue.

Conversation 3: Between You and the Enemy

Third, it's absolutely critical to acknowledge that you have a very real enemy, and he is very interested in how you use your words. He loves it when you use them to hurt people rather than heal them, to promote yourself instead of God.

After checking in with God and getting your self-talk truthfully reset, you'll do well to get into the habit of assessing the Enemy's level of access in a given situation. Are you about to communicate from a place of anger, hunger, exhaustion, exasperation, desperation, resignation, or fear? These postures are ripe for Satan's picking, so you might be better off keeping your mouth closed—at least until you've chilled out, settled down, eaten a snack, taken a nap, and moved in your attitude to a place of peace.

Conversation 4: Between You and Me

The fourth and final conversation is the one between you and me. Even after researching this book and practicing its tenets for more than two decades, I still find it astounding how kind, timely, and wise the words I speak to others can be when I'm faithful to steward the other three conversations well. Of course, that's probably because those words aren't completely my own but carry the weight of a higher influence—the One through whom all true healing and wisdom really come.

I want to speak words that gladden the heart of God. If you do too, then I invite you to read on.

PART ONE

THE CONVERSATION
BETWEEN YOU
AND GOD

1

THE SPEAKING GOD

*If you don't have clarity of ideas, you're just
communicating sheer sound.*

—Yo-Yo Ma

The most common question I get asked as a pastor—more frequently than why bad things happen to good people, why Christians are so hypocritical, and whether or not there will be sex in heaven—is this: *Does God really speak?* A full 100 percent of the time I'm asked this question, the inquirer isn't launching a theological debate but is asking for personal reasons. What people are really asking is "Does God really speak *to me?*"

For anyone who has spent any time around a Bible, it's pretty clear that God has spoken throughout history. He spoke through his Son, Jesus Christ—the "radiance of [God's] glory and the exact representation of His nature," the One who "upholds all things by the word of His power" (Heb. 1:3 NASB). Before that, God spoke through a parade of prophets—Isaiah, Jeremiah, Ezekiel, Daniel, and more.

He spoke to Moses "face to face, as one speaks to a friend" (Exod. 33:11), to Abraham, exhorting him to walk faithfully and blamelessly before him (see Gen. 17:1), and to Noah, a total of five times over the nine hundred fifty years of Noah's life (see Gen. 9:29). Chase communication all the way back to the beginning, in fact, and there you'll find a speaking God. The creation account is riddled with evidence along these lines:

- "God said, 'Let there be light'" (Gen. 1:3).
- "God said, 'Let there be a vault between the waters'" (v. 6).
- "God said, 'Let the water under the sky be gathered to one place'" (v. 9).
- "God said, 'Let the land produce vegetation'" (v. 11).
- "God said, 'Let there be lights in the vault of the sky to separate the day from the night'" (v. 14).
- "God said, 'Let the water teem with living creatures'" (v. 20).
- "God saw that it was good. God blessed [his creation] and said, 'Be fruitful and increase in number'" (vv. 21–22).
- "God said, 'Let the land produce living creatures according to their kinds'" (v. 24).
- "God said, 'Let us make mankind in our image'" (v. 26).
- "God blessed [Adam and Eve] and said to them, 'Be fruitful and increase in number; fill the earth and subdue it'" (v. 28).

- "God said [to Adam and Eve], 'I give you every
  seed-bearing plant on the face of the whole earth
  and every tree that has fruit with seed in it'"
  (v. 29).

From the start, it seems, God longed to be with his people, to commune with them and have conversations with those he created. And yet even on the heels of such a litany, we come away wondering, *Is this still true today?*

Yeah, God spoke to Moses, the thinking goes, *but will he talk to someone like me?*

GOD IS THERE

As I said, I get this "Does God really speak?" question a lot. I've heard it from professional women and devoted dads, from elderly widows and teenagers. The businessman who asked it with tears in his eyes—"Why won't God speak to me?"—nearly left me speechless. I put my hand on his shoulder and said the same thing I always say in response to this question: "He will. He *does.* He has! God has spoken to you already. He is speaking to you today. And he will speak to you throughout the course of your life. All you have to do is tune in and listen to what he has to say."

If you're older than twenty-five or thirty, you probably remember the car radios of old that could only be tuned manually. There was no digital tuner back then that would take you with precision to 102.7 or 99.1 or whichever radio station you were hunting for, and so you'd have to sit there for what felt like an eternity turning the little knob in microscopic increments until you hit broadcasting gold. You'd hear static, static, static, and more static, and then *bam*! "Song of the South" by Alabama would warble itself into clarity, and you'd grin, throw the truck into gear, and head off down the road.

The reason we were willing to go to such lengths to locate our favorite radio station was because we knew without a doubt that it was there; we just had to find it. As it relates to God speaking, we can have that same confidence—he is there and just needs to be found. On one hand, this ought to be very good news, for God says that whenever we come looking for him, we will find him; that when we get serious about finding him and want it more than anything else, he will make sure we won't be disappointed (see Jer. 29:13).

On the other hand, the news that he is there for us to find can seem like a cruel game of cat and mouse. Our pursuit leaves us exhausted and disillusioned after so many near misses. We come across verses like Isaiah 43:12, which confirms that God spoke, that he saved, that he told us what existed "long before these upstart gods appeared on the scene" (THE MESSAGE), and Malachi 3:6, which assures us that God himself will never change. While the sum of those concepts ought to be as straightforward as two plus two equaling four, we can't quite get our minds and hearts to concede that yes, God has spoken; yes, God still speaks; and yes, we serve a speaking God. We can't, that is, until that speaking God *actually speaks to us*.

THIS TIME IT'S PERSONAL

If you had visited First Assembly of God church in Jonesboro, Louisiana, on a Sunday morning, a Sunday evening, or a Wednesday evening anytime between, say, 1983 and 1989, you'd have found my mom, my brother, my sister, and me, four ducks in a row, always seated in the very same pew. Dad wouldn't have been there, because somehow he always escaped Mom's mandate that we go to church—a church that was, incidentally, a twenty-five-mile car ride away. The sole lucky duck in our family would instead stay home, put on comfortable clothes, and watch whatever sporting event happened to be on TV.

I didn't dislike going to church; I just didn't get all the hype about God. This was a Pentecostal church, which meant a lot of enthusiastic bouncing around, copious amounts of whooping and hollering, and an overemphasis on "experiencing God." One woman, who often sat in front of my family, had a very large bee-hive hairdo that she kept in place with dozens of bobby pins. One Sunday I counted sixty-four. Anyway, she'd really get going during worship services, flailing her head around as if she were a heavy-metal guitarist, and those bobby pins would start flying toward my head like heat-seeking missiles.

Still, despite the craziness that sometimes characterized the *ethos* of the congregation of my youth, at fifteen years of age, I stood at the altar one Wednesday night and experienced firsthand what all the fuss was about. I'd never doubted that the congregants of the First Assembly of God church were sincere in their beliefs that God was near, that he was speaking, and that he wanted a close-knit relationship with them. What didn't sit so easily was the idea that he wanted anything to do *with me*.

Lingering at the altar was a big deal in that church. People came forward after worship services to have leaders of the church pray for them—for healing, for protection, for provision, and more. Folks would hang out there for up to an hour, praying and talking and probably just basking in the afterglow of the emotionally stirring experience they'd just had. As I stood there that night receiving prayer, everyone around me faded out of view. I no longer saw my surroundings as they were. Instead, in my mind's eye I saw the Trinity—God pointing me to his Spirit, the Spirit pointing me to Jesus, Jesus pointing me back to the Father.

God was conveying his nearness to me, his interest in me, his desire to stay in touch. For a fifteen-year-old, this was huge—but then I suspect it's huge for us all, no matter how old we are, when such an awareness of God hits.

A few months ago at New Life, I met a woman named Anna and her three children. After exchanging pleasantries, she dove headlong into conversation about her spiritual journey and, specifically, about how, when she was about to enter the eighth grade, the Catholic priest at the church her family attended stood before a whole bunch of confirmation-class candidates—this woman included—and said, "Young men, young women, this choice to relate with God is yours to make. Nobody can make it for you."

Anna said, "This was news to me. First of all, I didn't know I had any say in my spiritual life. As far as I knew, religion got passed down to you from your parents, and I assumed that the obligations and regulations my parents abided by were going to be rails I'd have to run on too. But second, who knew a person could actually *relate* with God?"

I nodded. I've been there. We've all been there, I would guess, shocked by the realization that God has communicated with us, his most prized possessions, and that what he wants more than anything is for us to say something back.

I recounted for Anna an abbreviated version of my story of discovering God as a fifteen-year-old on my own terms, and as I spoke, I detected a little envy in her eyes.

"See, *that's* what I want for my kids," she said, motioning to the son and two daughters at her side. "I want to explain God to them so they don't have to go through what I went through—all the confusion and disillusion and all the rest."

She asked me to recommend some good books to buy her kids, or maybe a Christian curriculum to help them understand God, but partway through I interrupted her.

"Are you open to pursuing a different goal?" I asked.

She paused, jerked her head back a little, and said, "Than helping my kids understand God? I'm not sure I follow."

I told her I thought that by putting pressure on herself to "explain God" to her kids, she was setting her family up for failure. "It's too big a task for a parent to explain God to a child," I said. "And if that's your goal—to give your kids as many facts about God as possible—then won't you be doing the same thing to them that your parents did to you?"

A light went on in her eyes. "Right, right," she said. "Okay, then what? What is the goal?"

"What if you focus on helping your kids *discover God* instead— who he is, how he communicates, what he's after in their lives? Let them see you discovering God day by day, and then aid them in their own discovery. God can't be fully explained. But *encountered*? He's all over that."

She nodded, and a huge smile spread across her face.

Just as Anna did in that moment, we all need to realize that God is there—and that he longs to be found.

TURNING A DEAF EAR TO GOD

This idea that God speaks to his children makes perfect sense when we think of it like our parenting—the way in which we relate to our own kids. My wife, Pam, and I aren't big on rules at our house, aside from a few basics: tell the truth, don't sneak around, treat people the way you hope to be treated, and honor our God-given authority as Mom and Dad. Here's what we *are* big on: communication. We work hard to create an environment where unplanned, unrushed conversations are not the exception but the norm.

We study our kids daily so that we know the right times and the right approaches to draw them into dialogue with us. Why? So that we can help them pave viable lanes for traveling through life. Our words provide direction. They provide encouragement for the journey. They provide hints for avoiding roadblocks. They provide wisdom for steering clear of a crash. Time and again in Scripture, I see this very same theme pop up: God speaking to his children to save them from the world around them and from themselves.

One of the most popular Bible stories to trot out whenever the discussion centers on God connecting conversationally with mortals is that of the Old Testament prophet Samuel when he was just a boy. The backstory (found in 1 Samuel 1–2) is about an infertile woman named Hannah who begged God for a child, promising that if God granted her request in general and gave her a son in particular, she would dedicate that young man to the temple and set him apart for service to God. In those days, to devote a child to ministry meant turning him over to live with priests. Those elder statesmen would train him day and night, and he would virtually never leave their side. So God gave Hannah a son, and once he was the appropriate age, his adoring mother took him to the temple, introduced him to Eli, the high priest, and then bade him a fond farewell.

The text (see 1 Sam. 3:1–10) tells us that, at the time, God's revelation was rarely seen or heard, which may explain why neither Samuel *nor* Eli gathered that the One who interrupted Samuel's deep sleep one night was in fact almighty God. Three times God whispered, "Samuel! Samuel!" Three times Samuel answered, "Yes?" and rushed into Eli's room thinking it was he who had called. And three times Eli said, "I didn't call you. Go back to bed."

But before Samuel left Eli's presence the third time, it dawned on Eli that this could be *God* trying to communicate with the boy. So he gave Samuel some instructions. "The next time you hear the voice," Eli said, "just say, 'Speak, God, for your servant is listening.'"

A few minutes later, the voice called young Samuel's name a fourth time, and in response, Samuel did as he'd been told. "Speak," he said to God. "I'm your servant, ready to listen."

It's a popular story because it's a *beautiful* story—of how God reaches out to fallible people like us, of how those with listening ears can actually commune with the living God, and of how one eager, available servant can change the course of human history. But there's another reason the story packs a killer punch: it centers on *the message* God reached out to convey. See, God wasn't waking Samuel to tell him he loved him and thought he was great, although theologically both of those sentiments are true. Samuel was roused from a deep sleep because he was needed for the task of carefully communicating something to Eli. God told Samuel that night,

> I will carry out against Eli everything I spoke against his family—from beginning to end. For I told him that I would judge his family forever because of the sin he knew about; his sons blasphemed God, and he failed to restrain them. Therefore I swore to the house of Eli, "The guilt of Eli's house will never be atoned for by sacrifice or offering." (vv. 12–14)

Essentially, God was about to rain down judgment on Eli and Eli's family, and he wanted Samuel to deliver the final warning.

If we back up a chapter to 1 Samuel 2, we learn that not only were Eli's sons disrespecting people's offerings to God, but they were also sleeping with the hostesses who stood at the entrance to the tent of meeting where people came to worship God. The high priest's sons were doing this, and what's worse, the high priest did nothing about it. I saw a story recently detailing a trend among parents in which they go to great lengths to make sure their teenagers are comfortable sleeping with a boyfriend or girlfriend right there under their own roofs. When a seventeen-year-old daughter asked her mother if the girl's boyfriend could sleep over, not only did the mom say yes, but she went out and bought her daughter a bigger bed![1]

This is the type of negligent oversight Eli was about to be judged for, and according to God, that judgment wasn't going to be fun. But what I want you to catch is that God went *around* Eli to communicate something *to* Eli, which ought to tell us something *about* Eli: *he no longer had ears to hear.*

The text tells us that Eli tried to rebuke his sons once, but they disregarded their dad. God had warned Eli to rectify the situation or his entire family would suffer (see vv. 30–33), to which Eli simply turned a deaf ear. Eli was accustomed to religious ritual and had grown up around talk of God his entire life, but now the One he'd centered his life around couldn't have gotten his attention with a megaphone. The high priest whose job it was to offer the people salvation was himself refusing to be saved.

SALVATION, AGAIN AND AGAIN

That supernatural encounter I had when I was fifteen proved instrumental in my pursuit of God. For the first time in my young life, it felt as if God had reached out not just to humanity in general, as I'd been taught, but to me, Brady Boyd, in particular. I wanted to respond to him. I knew he was saying something to me—something that sounded like love. I wanted what God was offering me—acceptance, relationship, and grace, yes—but also, as I'd soon come to discover, protection from the world and from myself.

At the time, I attended a very sexualized high school. I'm not sure sex could have been a bigger deal if the administrators had written it into the curriculum—maybe if they'd *encouraged* promiscuity, the cool kids wouldn't have found it cool. The fact was, though, the cool kids *did* think it was cool, and the message I received from my friends every day encouraged me to have sex as often as possible with as many different girls as possible so I would fit in.

Of course I wanted to fit in, but there was that encounter I'd had with God. I didn't know anything about theology or soteriology (i.e., the study of salvation) or all the ways sin muffles the voice of God. All I knew was that the guys having sex every weekend never talked about God and didn't seem to care whether he was trying to talk to them. I had all the same inclinations every other teenage boy seems to have, but something in me knew that if I wanted to build on the thing I had going with God, then I couldn't also be the guy having unmarried sex.

Most weekends, while everyone I knew was hanging out at parties and hooking up with girls, I would hunt, fish, or go horseback riding with my brother, or take long walks alone. I'd pray during those walks—at least as much as I knew how. Nothing earth-shattering happened as a result of those prayers, but I did sense God's companionship. I knew he was with me and that he cared.

When the days started to get longer as winter eased into spring, I'd be outside until nine at night, soaking up backwoods Louisiana and the adventures she always provided. And then I'd make my way home, where I'd watch TV or just sit and talk to my parents for a while. After that I'd head to bed.

When I was a junior, a group of seniors—all girls—started convening by my locker, and one day a couple of them began to flirt with me. This group wasn't exactly known for upright behavior. Moral integrity wasn't their claim to fame. Despite being a teenage male, all of whom are pretty much governed by raging hormones and an undeveloped prefrontal cortex, I remember their come-ons sliding off me like water off a duck's slick back. I'd been marked by a series of spiritual experiences so deeply fulfilling—that night at the altar and dozens of prayer walks through the woods—that by comparison, all else was a cheap knockoff.

Nothing matched the satisfaction I felt whenever I felt connected to God. And to me, that's exactly the point of divine conversation: each time we allow God to talk us away from temptation, we find salvation all over again—salvation from perishing, salvation from bondage, salvation from addiction, salvation from pain. When we're willing to trust the guidance of our Father, our path is one of blessing, freedom, and hope.

This idea that God's input always leads his people toward spiritual, emotional, and physical productivity was even at the heart of the Law God gave his people. Think about it: Did God give them the Ten Commandments just to be mean and kill their fun? Or did he offer the commandments as a template for them to follow, in essence saying, "These guidelines are your only hope for success"? He *adored* the nation of Israel, even choosing them intentionally, as you'll recall, from all others on the earth at the time. And because of his great devotion to them, he spoke brilliant words of light into the darkness of their hearts.

WHAT GOD ALWAYS SAYS

My motivation for pursuing God seemed noble enough when I was fifteen, sixteen, seventeen years of age. I wanted to relate with him. I wanted to know what he thought about the decisions I was making in life. Increasingly, I wanted to hear from him before I made those decisions. Something was developing between God and me, something increasingly valuable. But then the bottom fell out of our relationship.

At my high school, the fact that I was taking a stand for God was all that much weightier because I was an athlete. In my hometown, a high school sports star was the ultimate celebrity. Entering my junior year of high school, all I could dream about was making the men's varsity basketball team.

The doctor's appointment was supposed to have been a routine preseason checkup, an insignificant checkpoint in my stellar career, a formality at most. I had a congenital heart condition, but it had never really interfered with daily life before that point.

"It's interfering now, though," I remember the doctor telling my mom. Those words rocked my world so hard that I remember wanting to puke.

According to my cardiologist, should my parents allow me to continue playing basketball, they would be putting my life in grave danger. He used those exact words: *grave danger*. That this guy actually thought basketball was going to kill me proved he wasn't playing with a full deck. I never felt more alive than when I was on a hardwood court—but that was about to change forever.

My mom and I left that appointment and headed home. I fumed the entire drive. I wasn't angry with the doctor who had just unilaterally killed my athletic career. I wasn't frustrated with my parents, even though I knew they'd been swayed by the doc's advice. The one I was furious with was God. I'd trusted him, and he'd let me down. The truths I cling to today—that God is forever vying for my peace and purity, that he's a loving Father who purposes good for my life—I didn't buy into that day.

It all seemed like a cruel, crushing joke. How could I love a God who's willing to let something so small smash my greatest hopes? So instead of trusting him, I cut off all communication with him. I turned my back on him and decided to go my own way. Despite all the good he had done in me up to that point, that day I decided I no longer had room for him in my life.

There's an interesting story in Scripture about a son who cut off all communication with his father, turned his back on his father's will, and went his own way in a huff (see Luke 15:11–32). Maybe the reason it has always been my favorite story is because of that plot's striking resemblance to my own: I too wandered into a desert season, eventually realized the error of my ways, and then desperately craved the goodness of going home again. This much I know: the scene that gets me every time is when the offended father embraces the offending son the moment the prodigal returns to him.

The father's kindness was totally undeserved. The man's son had been prideful, presumptuous, disrespectful, wasteful—any way you slice it, he'd been a jerk. He blew through his inheritance, the money he'd insisted on taking even before his father died, and then, after burning through all other options, he landed on the audacious idea of returning home, looking the man he'd so disrespected straight in the eyes and asking for his forgiveness.

I try to put myself in that dad's shoes, and "kindness" feels like a stretch. As a parent facing a kid behaving irresponsibly, wouldn't you have to sermonize a little? Say, "I told you so"?

Granted, the son was planning to humble himself before his father (i.e., ask for a job among the servants) once he was back home. He'd even rehearsed his spiel: "Father, I've sinned against God, I've sinned before you; I don't deserve to be called your son. Take me on as a hired hand" (vv. 18–19 THE MESSAGE). He was going to apologize and do his best to make things right, but before he could get the words out, his father had something to say. After barking a series of good-natured orders—"Bring a clean set of clothes! Put the family ring on his finger! Fresh sandals, now! And while you're at it, our best grain-fed cow!"—the father announces to everyone within earshot, "My son! My son is *here*!" (vv. 22–24, paraphrased).

The day of that doctor's appointment, I walked away from God and didn't look back until the summer before my senior year of college. That summer it occurred to me that I had only one more year of school before I was on my own. Pam and I had met by then—we'd been dating two years already, in fact—and I was overwhelmed by the prospect of graduating from college, most likely marrying this wonderful woman, working to land my first real job, and trying to do all those things while holding on to the poisonous bitterness toward God that was eating away at my heart. I wasn't a teenager anymore; I was becoming a man. I'd gained a little maturity since the day I walked away from God, and now that I was coming to my senses, *I desperately wanted to go home.*

Like the Prodigal Son, I'd been prideful and wasteful and undisciplined and more, treating my college campus as if it was my own carnal playground. I'd picked up unhelpful habits, addictions, and propensities that I knew were offensive to God, but something deep in my soul knew he'd still run toward me in the same way that father ran toward his wandering son: "When [the son] was still a long way off, his father saw him. His heart pounding, [the father] ran out, embraced him, and kissed him" (v. 20 THE MESSAGE). I knew enough of God to realize that despite the coldhearted things I'd done, his reception would be warm. Why? Because despite my arrogance and willfulness, if I was honest about it, he still spoke to me, saying,

> *I'm here, and I love you, child.*
> *I'm ready to talk whenever you are.*

This is what God *always* communicates to us: that he is near and speaking and hopeful beyond belief that we'll come near and say something back.

Later that same summer—the summer I celebrated my twenty-first birthday and thus, in society's eyes anyway, became a man—I decided to go all in with God. I was weary of all the running, all the hustling, all the self-inflicted pain. So in August 1988, there in the driver's seat of my car, I told God he could be God. A cynic might say, "Gee, I'm sure God was relieved by your vote of confidence in him," but the sarcasm would be misplaced. The truth is that God *was* relieved by my vote of confidence, as he is when any of his children decide to quit running, to quit hustling, to quit hurting themselves, and to come home.

God is near us. He is interested in us. His desire is to stay in touch with us. But he won't bulldoze the barriers we've erected. No, he insists that *we* knock down those fortified walls ourselves.

Draw near to me, God always says to his children, *and I'll draw near to you. I've spoken. Will you say something back?*

TUNING IN | CHAPTER 1
Respond

1. Describe a time when you suspected that God was "out there" trying to communicate with you. What did you suppose he wanted to say?

2. What associations does the phrase *relating with God* bring to mind for you? What experiences have informed those thoughts?

3. What emotional or spiritual walls have you erected along the way in an attempt to keep God's business and your business distinct?

Reflect

Spend a few minutes reflecting on God's invitation to you, as noted at the end of the chapter. He is here. He loves you. And he's ready to talk whenever you are. What fears or insecurities surface in your heart as you consider such an invitation?

Read On

Look up the full story of the parable of the prodigal son found in Luke 15:11–32. How does the father's reaction to the prodigal relate to how you envision God's posture toward you whenever you're far from home?

2
STATIC

A man can no more diminish God's glory by refusing
to worship Him than a lunatic can put out the sun by
scribbling the word "darkness" on the walls of his cell.
—C. S. Lewis, *The Problem of Pain*

If the most common question I receive from people is "Does God really speak (to me)?" then the question that tends to directly follow is "*Then why can't I hear what he says?*"

Often the people asking this question have bottomed out and are pretty fired up about hearing God's voice. They blew their bonus checks and now are broke for the umpteenth time. They swore off booze, only to stock up at the liquor store again and go on a binge. They determined in their hearts to quit trolling the Internet late at night for technology's version of intimacy, and yet there they are again, sucked into the digital haze.

They've tried every other solution they can think of for solving whatever problem plagues them and have come up short, so now they're coming to Jesus. They're leaning in. They're slowly turning that radio knob, desperate to make out some semblance of clarity on the dial. They listen. They listen harder. They listen harder still. And yet, *nothing*. They hear only frustrating, mind-numbing static. "What gives?" they want to know. "Why can't I hear God's voice?" God seems distant and disinterested despite the sure sense somewhere deep inside them that God just *has* to be out there; he *has* to have something to say.

WE'RE THE ONES WHO MOVED

A while back, Abram and I were sitting in the hot tub, gazing at the stars and talking about God. My son's a hard-core thinker, a ponderer, which means that pretty much everything the kid asks me catches me off guard. "Dad," he said, "do you ever doubt that God exists?"

I love that he asked me that question—*me*, a professional Christ follower, someone who gets paid to have faith in God.

I answered him honestly: "Yes, I do. I've gone through seasons of serious doubt, and I'm sure I'll go through more."

I recounted some of those doubt-drenched seasons for him. A set of awful circumstances showed up one time, and I wondered why God allowed them in my life. Relational tensions felt insurmountable, and I got shaky in my beliefs, finding the claims of Christ—hope, peace, restoration, reunion—way too good to be true. People I knew had stumbled upon successes that I desperately wanted for myself, and I got frustrated with God. Hadn't I done enough right things in exchange for a little blessing too? I was saying all this when I noticed my son's shoulders relax and heard him sigh.

"What, you thought I never doubted God?" I asked him.

"All I know is I have those thoughts sometimes," he replied, "and I feel guilty about them whenever I do."

The truth is that we all doubt God's presence and power from time to time, and for good reason: If he's so near, why can't we sense him? If he's so caring, why do we get lonely and afraid? If he's so chatty, why does it seem like he's silent? If he's so eager to relate with us, why doesn't he just make himself known?

What unfolded between Abram and me that night is a version of nearly every conversation I have with those who ask me why they can't hear the voice of God. And I always have some version of the same response. In short, when God seems so far away that we're incapable of hearing his voice, he isn't the One who moved; we're the ones who created the distance. (There are times when God is silent to teach us to walk by faith rather than sight, but what I'm talking about here is the distance we create by disconnecting from him.) The themes of the Scriptures confirm that *God longs to stay intimately connected with us* throughout the course of our days. Why? Because he knows that apart from him we can't accomplish what he has asked us to do. We need his encouragement. We need his empowerment. We need his emboldening presence. We need the resources only he can provide.

Listen, we can't love well when we're disconnected from God. We can't serve well when we're disconnected from God. We can't say a *single fitting word* when we're living disconnected from God. *Nothing* in life works as it should when the lines between God and us have been clipped, which is why that father in the parable of the prodigal son celebrated with abandon when his child returned home. The moment we quit running from God and turn to have a conversation with him instead, the gears that were gummed up get greased and recalibrated and start humming along once again.

Before we look at what that "recalibrated" relationship with God looks like, though, let's shoot straight about the three main ways we tend to run from him.

DISTRACTION

At last check, you and I are receiving upward of five thousand marketing messages a day, which promote everything from online gambling to new cars to the mammoth fast-food cheeseburger that somehow relates to the scantily clad blonde bombshell being used to promote it. "It's a non-stop blitz of advertising messages," says Jay Walker-Smith, who runs a London-based marketing firm. Marketers now plaster corporate logos and taglines on everything from escalator handrails to jetliner fuselages to the sides of buildings to big-city sidewalks. There was even talk at one point of using Major League Baseball bases to promote upcoming movies! According to Walker-Smith, "It's all an assault on the senses."[1]

He's absolutely right.

I was in New York City a few weeks ago to help celebrate the fourteenth anniversary of the church some friends planted just months after 9/11. I was in town to encourage them and their congregation, but when I discovered I had a four-hour block of unassigned time on Saturday afternoon, I couldn't resist the chance to take in a few Manhattan sights. I eventually wound up in Central Park, thinking I'd find a quiet corner where I could sit, think, and maybe pray for a few minutes. At least I could simply reflect on the season of life I'm in.

I wandered around the massive tangle of plots and trails for probably ten minutes before I realized there is no such thing as a "quiet corner" in Central Park. That night when I reconvened with my friends, I told them about my afternoon and then asked, "Where do you guys find silence in this town? The streets are loud, the inside of my hotel room is loud, and even Central Park, for all its beauty, is, I'm convinced, one of the loudest places on Earth."

They chuckled and said, "Brady, we've learned to thrive in the chaos. You would too if you lived here."

It's the mantra of an entire society now, this idea that we can actually thrive amid chaos, even as we're not really thriving at all. Most of us are a restless people, incapable of stilling ourselves— mind, body, *or* soul. I asked my congregation to sit in perfect silence one Sunday to prove to them how uncomfortable we've become when the noise dies down, the lights quit blinding us, and we're left with the company of our own thoughts. It was only fifteen seconds, but I could sense the jitters by the end.

I've said it before and I'll say it again: we are busier than we're meant to be. We're letting our senses get assaulted by what we see and what we hear, the net effect of which is our inability to detect the voice of God. We don't see him in the world around us. We don't hear him over the unceasing roar of our lives. Then we come away thinking that *he's* the problem, that he's abandoned us to ourselves. The hard pill to swallow is that our addiction to chaos is what's keeping us from God—or one of the top things, anyway. If we're serious about encountering him, we'll get serious about quieting our souls.

If you grew up in certain circles, you're familiar with the phrase *quiet time*. In the Pentecostal church of my youth, everybody was big on having a daily quiet time, which was the twenty or thirty minutes you were to spend reading your Bible, praying, and getting yourself centered for the day ahead. It may sound antiquated, but now more than ever I think we'd benefit from setting aside a daily quiet time, if for no other reason than to actually practice being quiet.

My advice to you if you're struggling and straining to hear the voice of God: *be quiet.* Schedule a quiet time and just sit there in a chair, with nothing in your hands and no earbuds in your ears. Just get quiet before God and see what unfolds. Start small. Start microscopically if you have to. *Just start.*

Whenever I'm back in Louisiana, I morph into a full-on naturalist, someone who feels most at home, say, out in the woods. It was there my conversations with God started when I was dipping my toe into spiritual waters partway through my teenage years. And it's there I sense his presence most powerfully as I traipse along those same trails as a grown man. Even hiking in Colorado can take me back to that spiritually rich environment—I get outside and away from technological devices, and I can smell the trees of the Deep South. I can hear the wind that whooshes across Louisianan lakes and swamps. I can see the birds that dive-bomb from overhead cloud formations. I can taste the pungency that always floats in the air.

Outside, in nature, I'm reminded that God is big and I am not, that God is whole and I am not, that God is holy and I am not—although by his Spirit, I'm getting there. Outside, with an abundance of breathtaking vistas and a scarcity of distractions, I'm able to better hear my Father's voice—the one that two decades ago welcomed me back into his loving arms. There were no lectures. There were no sermons. There was no "I told you so." Just a whooping, hollering, "My son! My son is *here!*" It's all good parents ever really want—the kids they adore close by. And so, back to my advice: put down your phone and your iPad, close your computer, turn off your TV, and silence the radio, signaling that entertainment is not your god. Come before your doting Father with open hearts, hands, and ears. And then welcome the work of his Spirit, who wants to commune with you today.

STUBBORN INDEPENDENCE

Pam and I have lived in Colorado for almost a decade, and while living here, we've picked up on the undeniable characteristic of Coloradans that we've come to call "rugged independence." This is a feisty, no-fluff, can-do attitude that wouldn't ask for help if lives depended on it. This poses a problem when the subject is God, though, given that his entire grace-fueled invitation is predicated on a supernatural and perfect being offering divine and penetrating aid to carnal, imperfect souls. You know what Coloradans say to an offer like that? "I'm managing fine on my own here, but thanks for dropping by."

Managing fine on our own is a life strategy set in complete opposition to the way of Christ—and it's doing us no favors along the way. Our lives get sideways because our relationships get sideways. Our relationships get sideways because our conversations get sideways. Those conversations get sideways because our words are sometimes unwise and because they flow from hearts not experiencing full surrender to God. Coloradans aren't much for fully surrendering to *anything* except their own ideas, instincts, and plans. (And the truth of the matter is that most Americans are like that—Coloradans are just more blatant about it.)

People who know me well know that I'm a devoted Louisiana State University (LSU) football fan. Some tell me they block my Twitter feed for half the year, explaining that from August until clear after the New Year, I'm "obnoxious" in my support of my Tigers. I find that descriptor a little harsh, though. I can't help that I'm so passionate, I always try to explain to those friends. The purple and gold get into a person's blood! Still, they're never persuaded. Culture is an inside job.

One of the little-known aspects of LSU folklore is that for every roar heard on game day from the LSU mascot, Mike the Tiger (the real tiger, not the guy wandering the sidelines in the costume of a tiger), the football team will score one touchdown. One roar equals one touchdown. Three roars equal three touchdowns. Six roars, and it's the 2011 blowout against Auburn at home. Anyway, when you arrange your Saturday activities around the television broadcasts of LSU football games—as I've been known to do—you pick up handy bits of information like this.

I learned in the same segment that talked about the roars-to-scores ratio that there is an entire cult following for Mike the Tiger, and even his costumed counterpart, also named Mike the Tiger, has a full entourage that helps him care for his costume, dress for games, get to games and events on time, and make a good showing each January at the Disney World mascot competition. (I'm being serious. You can't make this stuff up.) The entourage is named Team Mike.

As I sat there listening to this whole spiel, which included plentiful cutaway footage of the cartoon tiger jumping around, making people laugh, and in general being the life of the party, I thought about how entertaining mascots are hilarious and harmless and fun. Then I thought about how tempting it is—spiritually speaking—to want not a Messiah but a mascot, a silent guarantor of weekly good luck. I don't doubt Team Mike's care for their beloved mascot, and I don't at all doubt that their devotion is true, but I can hardly conceive of a situation whereby Mike is consulted about the game's actual strategy or play calling.

Mike is just a symbol; he holds no real authority or sway. Something about that feels way too familiar. It feels a lot like the way we adorn ourselves with all things Jesus but never let him be the Lord in our lives. Too often we're not really followers; we're just fans.

This realization sank in as the camera cut to the costumed Mike delighting the crowd with cartwheels, stopping to pose for a picture, and dancing out of the camera shot to the rhythms pounding through the stadium's giant speakers. Members of Team Mike surrounded the mascot, held up brightly painted signs, and together chanted the well-known sentiment "Geaux, Tigers! Geaux!"

And all the while a single thought wound its way through my mind: if we're not careful, those of us who say we love God and are committed to living for him will devolve into Team Jesus, a flighty group of fans who want a mute talisman who cheers us up, —a mascot we never really see as anything more than someone to rally around for fun, not the divisive Savior who comes to separate wheat from chaff.

Why would we hear from God if we don't really feel we need him? We think we're managing fine on our own—and not just here in Colorado, I should note. As I said before, most everywhere I visit, I see a similar ruggedly independent spirit, wide swaths of the population who get a kick out of all things Jesus but refuse to surrender to him.

There is one exception to this trend worth mentioning, and it's found in places where resources are thin. I've visited the least resourced parts of Guatemala and Kenya and even these great United States, and the common denominator yoking them all together is their hunger for intervention from God. They recognize their need for God acutely because they are so clear on the fact that they have nothing else giving them life. This is a far cry from many North American pantries, which are stuffed with six months' worth of food. When you eat as much food as you want on a given day, you're less likely to hunger for God. Haven't you discovered this to be true in your own life? When you're in want, you want God more.

I talk with successful businessmen and businesswomen about these ideas from time to time, and the look they give me in return says, "What, you want me to take a vow of poverty?" to which I give a look that says, "Just hear me out." Resources in and of themselves are not evil; it's simply that when we come to believe we're managing our food supply and our housing and our vocational world and our relationships "just fine on our own," we inadvertently tune to static on the airwaves of our lives.

What if instead of signing up for static, we voluntarily reduced the noise level in our lives and patiently tuned in to God? What if instead of cooking up our own sustenance day by day, we waited on the divine provision he says he'll give us? I wonder if our conversations would be more plentiful then, and we'd finally start to hear from heaven.

We take Communion most weeks at New Life, a practice that has quickly become my favorite part of the entire service. The elements of bread and wine—or juice, as the case may be— remind me of Christ's great sacrifice: his body broken, his blood spilled out, his vast love for me as his son. The bread also makes me think about the part of the Lord's Prayer that says we should ask God for our "daily bread," for sustenance along this journey of life. Whenever I bite into that tiny, crunchy wafer, I realize afresh that I'm generally at my holiest, most-whole self just after I partake.

Right after Communion, I am a person at peace—*perfect* peace. Whatever was irritating me or distracting me before Communion is momentarily suspended by the sheer force of communing with Love, with Grace. Right after Communion I'm relaxed. I'm calm. I'm at rest. And I'm kind. By the time I close the service and step out of the auditorium, my irritations and distractions start vying for my attention again, which is why I'm so vulnerable in those moments to the opinionated rants of others. But *immediately after* Communion, God has his way in my life.

That makes me wonder, what if this Communion "carriage" could be true of me all the time? What if I carried myself with peace and grace and kindness not just on the heels of the sacrament but on Monday through Saturday too? What if *you* did the same? Can you imagine the good that would do?

We say the wrong thing so much of the time because we're trying to satisfy our craving for the bread of heaven with the cheap-flour imitations of earth. In essence Jesus says, "Ask *me* for your daily bread to survive what this day will hold," to which we say, "Nah, but thanks for the offer, Jesus. I'll just whip up some loaves on my own."

It's like Jesus saying to us, "Abide in me, and I'll abide in you, and you'll keep yourself out of trouble and your foot out of your mouth," to which we grin in patronizing fashion, thinking, *That Jesus. He's a persistent one. Doesn't he know I've already kneaded the dough?*

I can always tell when I'm refusing to feast on the sustenance Jesus offers, preparing provisions on my own instead. I overreact; I fire back half cocked; I power up over someone I'm called to lead; I try to pocket my sinfulness, hoping God isn't looking and therefore won't see. I say and do any of a thousand things, all in the name of nourishing myself. God whispers my way in an attempt to catch my attention, to speak to me, to offer me some direction and help, but I don't hear a word of it over the clanging in the kitchen, where I'm baking my own bread.

But the flip side is equally true. Whenever the bread of heaven sates my appetite, I tend toward spiritual sanity in every aspect of life: my actions reveal levelheadedness, my posture reveals peace, my words reveal wisdom, and my *entire being* is rooted in Christ. I come to every conversation as a person whose core needs have been met, which means I don't need another person to resolve any deep-seated ache in my heart. That ache has been set right in God, and now I can engage fully, freely, without any static cluttering my thoughts.

DISOBEDIENCE

The third—and perhaps most blatant—way you and I tend to run from God is outright disobedience. We who say we want to hear from God usually mean that we want to hear from God *except* when what he says gets in the way of what we want to do. This was at the heart of my years-long cold shoulder toward God, and based on hundreds of conversations week in and week out with people from every conceivable background and walk of life, I believe it remains the biggest dilemma a human being can face. We want God's will, but we want to maintain a will of our own. God says, *Pick one.*

To which we say, *Fine. I pick mine.*

I was teaching at New Life one Sunday and mentioned from the platform that I had spoken at a church in another state the week before. Later, after I dismissed the congregation, a young woman who was very pregnant came rushing up to me and said with great energy and effusiveness, "You have connections to the South? We just moved here from there!"

A man I presumed was her husband and also a cute child about age two or three sidled up to the woman as she continued. "We are so excited to have found New Life! Especially now that we know that you have ties to our home state."

I told her it was great to meet her and then, as I offered a handshake to the man, asked her, "Is this your husband?"

She replied, "Oh! Yes. Yes! And … funny story about us. He proposed marriage to me the same day my water broke with our first child!" She then fell apart in a wave of giggles, while the husband and I grinned awkwardly at each other.

Men don't know what to do when women start talking about water breaking, but there was more to my awkwardness than that. I try to be wholly accepting of anyone and everyone I meet, and in my heart of hearts, I held no judgment toward this lovely family. Still, the thought that occurred to me was this: *Thirty years ago, a newcomer to a church would never have admitted to the pastor— unabashedly, unashamedly, and with such enthusiasm, no less—that she'd had a baby out of wedlock.*

Such things just didn't happen.

I felt no spirit of judgment rise up in me toward that family. Rather, I felt a spirit of judgment rise up in me toward our culture and the perilous shift we've allowed. Ironically, I found her candor and authenticity refreshing—*She's telling me this? In our very first conversation? At church?* And yet I couldn't swat away the sinking sense that we, as a people, have veered way off God's desired course.

Rebellion and disobedience are in the air.

Collectively we've decided to go our own way in life and then say to anyone and everyone we happen upon, "I'm great with how this all unfolded in my life. Why wouldn't you be great with it too?"

I do this too, of course—this me-myself-and-I approach to life. God says, *This is the way, Brady. Walk in it* (see Isa. 30:21). To which I respond, *Can "the way" include just this one quick detour? And this one? Oh, and this one over here as well?*

I go my own direction—deliberately—and then ask God to bless wherever it is I've arrived as a result. My desires and motivations can be that strong, even as a pastor. Like the apostle Paul's timeless lament in Romans 7, I don't *want* to behave this way, but then I find myself doing just that, time and again. I convey basically the same sentiment to God that that pregnant woman conveyed to me: *I'm great with how everything is unfolding, God. Why can't you just be great with it too?*

I make my own decisions and then ask God to retroactively make them pure. I want God to speak into my life, except when that input gets in the way of what I want.

You'll recall that God offered this same proposition to Eve and Adam in the garden of Eden: "Walk with me. Listen to me. Trust me, my daughter, my son. No self-won pleasure can come close to eclipsing the joy you'll know when you and I are sojourning in peace."

God wanted close proximity with them, but they wanted their own pursuits for pleasure more. So they disobeyed the instructions God provided for them and sinned against the One they loved.

Later that sin-stained day, in the cool of the late afternoon, when God came around for their sunset walk, the disobedient ones were nowhere to be found. And one of the most devastating scenes in all of Scripture reveals what happened next.

> When [Adam and Eve] heard the sound of GOD strolling in the garden in the evening breeze, the Man and his Wife hid in the trees of the garden, hid from GOD. GOD called to the Man: "Where are you?" (Gen. 3:8–9 THE MESSAGE)

"I made you to enjoy my fellowship," God must have murmured incredulously, "to walk with me through this thing called life. I breathed existence into your lungs and provided for you everything you could possibly need—protection and sustenance, challenges to engage you, body and mind. I love you with an ever-lasting love, a type of love you can't find anywhere else. But here I am, eager to talk with you, ready to invest in our mutual bond, and your actions betray your hearts' posture toward me. You want nothing to do with me. Where are you, Daughter? Where are you, Son? What has stolen your affection for me?"

I can't even imagine what that must have felt like.

A man I know is married and has five children. He is a solid, upstanding guy. Along the way he and I have had brief but meaningful conversations about his professional world, his hobbies, his family, and his desire to faithfully follow God. I was impressed with the perspicacity of his decision making, with how he led his company, his loved ones, and himself.

He was on a business trip not long ago. Because of a weather-related dinner-meeting cancellation, he wound up with a big chunk of free time on his hands. He meandered down to the hotel restaurant and was told there was a thirty-minute wait. So he decided to hang out at the bar. He ordered a drink and then decided he'd have another, even though this was uncharacteristic for him. He drank the second and ordered a third—unheard of in this man's paradigm.

After downing the third drink, his mind now reeling and his senses dulled, he decided to bypass dinner in favor of heading for bed. But once he reached his hotel room upstairs, he gravitated toward his laptop instead, and twenty minutes later, he found himself flirting with a fifteen-year-old girl in an online chat room, a wild departure from the course he'd been on for the entirety of his adult life.

The young woman eagerly agreed to meet him—"just to talk," they confirmed—but when the man arrived at the designated meeting place, he discovered he'd been corresponding not with a hot young thing but with a sheriff's deputy.

God wants close proximity to us, but we want to pursue our pleasures more.

As an aside, it's popular to rave about the amount of technology available to us, as though we've reached some sort of utopia at last, but given the portals we can now enter—with a simple swipe or click, no less—our lives can change in an instant. What we believed would simplify our lives has made them more complex, because whenever we're isolated or lonely or momentarily detached from our core values, the opportunity to sneak around digitally seems like a reasonable option.

I travel a lot, just as this guy did, and I sense my vulnerability the moment I take even one step away from my primary sources of accountability and the typical rhythms that keep me tethered to God. I get in my car to head to the airport, to fly off alone to one destination or another, thinking, *Brady, be on your guard. God is with you, but your enemy is stalking you. Follow Boyd Family Rule Numero Uno: Do not sneak around.*

Well, within moments of the businessman's arrival at the meeting place, the deputy had cuffed him and was reading him his rights. As she led him to her unmarked cruiser and helped him into the caged backseat, he saw in his mind's eye the faces of his wife and young children, staring at him dumbfounded. He would be denied visits with those beloved children for a full six months' time, given his new status as a sexual predator, a criminal threat to his own kids in the law's eyes. He lost his job, which financially ruined him, and he still hasn't been able to land new work because of what a background check now reveals. He's never had extra-marital sex with anyone—underage or otherwise—but a single sneaking-around decision effectively destroyed his life.

I've seen him on occasion and asked him how things are going. "I'll be lucky to work the drive-through lane at a fast-food restaurant now," he said to me, tears springing to his eyes. His wife has stayed with him and is always there by his side, but her countenance is now one of disillusionment—of trust in and respect for her husband long since destroyed.

For weeks after the man shared what had happened, I couldn't shake the image of God—the God who is in us by his Spirit, and with us, around us, and for us—softly whispering with each key-stroke the man typed that night, *Son, I'm here for our evening walk.*

Son?

Where are you, Son?

Even writing about that man's story makes me want to puke. Disobedience can be so seductive, can't it? And then—*Pow!*—in an instant, life changes ... and that change is never for the good.

Of course, the disobedience that keeps us from hearing the voice of God doesn't have to be this egregious, or even something we do. There are things we do that are wrong, but there are also good things we should do that we don't. I've been guilty of both along the way. For example, on the heels of the tragic shooting on our campus that took the lives of two of our congregation's young girls in 2007, I walked through the toughest two years of ministry I've ever known.

Our entire church was suffering, and on most days I was fighting to survive. To make matters worse, despite my fervent efforts to reach God through Bible reading, prayer, and the wise counsel of pastors and friends, all I was getting from heaven was straight radio silence—nothing more.

Those days were incredibly frustrating as I banged on God's front door … until I realized that he'd already spoken to me. I was just refusing to do what he'd said.

Many years prior, during a quiet time with the Lord, he sealed a verse in my mind and heart that would direct my ministry endeavors for decades to come. The verse was James 1:27, which says, "Religion that God our Father accepts as pure and faultless is this: to look after orphans and widows in their distress and to keep oneself from being polluted by the world." I'd read and reread that verse, I'd memorized it, and I'd preached on the fact that those words were my official "life verse," and yet during the darkest moments of my ministry, I'd forgotten what that verse instructed me to do.

What God said to me through his radio silence was, *Brady, I've already given you my opinion on what I'd like for you to do. I won't be saying anything further until you decide to do those things.*

I now know that whenever I can't hear the voice of God, it would serve me well to review the last input I received from him to see whether I've tied up all the loose ends. A loving parent of a preschooler knows that if that child has been asked to brush her teeth at bedtime and has chosen not to comply, further input should be given only after that first gate has been cleared. "Are your teeth clean? Great. Now let's pick out a book to read." What that "teeth cleaning" looked like for me was going back to my original, God-given mission and completing that assignment first.

So as a church, we opened a health clinic for underinsured moms; we launched an effort to find every orphan in the care of the State of Colorado a loving Christian home; and we purchased and renovated an apartment complex so that single moms and their children would have a safe, clean place to live rather than living on the streets or in the backs of their cars. Only then could I expect God to chat with me again—only after I'd fulfilled the instructions he'd already sent my way.

The nation of Israel once famously responded to God's loving input with stubbornness and self-focused demands, telling God they wanted a king. Up to that point in history, God led the Israelites through his prophets and a series of judges he'd appointed to rule on his behalf. But God's leadership was becoming bothersome to his people, so they decided to go their own way. "Make us a king to judge us like all the nations!" they said, their fists raised in opposition to God (see 1 Sam. 8:5).

God warned them what would happen if he installed an earthly king. The king would reign over them, conscript their husbands and sons for military service, make them laborers for his cause, and take the best of their possessions to redistribute them to his staff. "You will cry out for relief from the king you have chosen," God told the Israelites through the prophet Samuel, "but the LORD will not answer you in that day" (v. 18).

"Let me be your king," God was begging them. "Don't insist on going your own way. I've promised to preserve and protect you. I have your best interests at heart."

But the nation of Israel—God's chosen people, no less— wanted nothing to do with such talk. They'd resolved in their hearts the path they were determined to take, and nothing could stop them now.

"We don't want your leadership, God. We want to be cool, like everyone else. We despise your authority in our lives. Step aside. Let us do our own thing."

So God gave them a king—and the devastating effects of their decision unfolded, just as God had wisely foretold.

I think about those Israelites whenever I find myself irritated with God. Things never go well for me when I kick against his will and his ways. Truly, I can't run toward him when I'm preoccupied with running away. I can't hear from him when I'm so far out of range. And so, whether my disobedience looks like outright rebellion or negligence in carrying out his plans, I do well to clean up my act each and every time I realize I've strayed from the path he'd have me on.

REVELATION WE URGENTLY NEED

In John 16, Jesus was preparing his disciples for his departure and for the arrival of the Holy Spirit of God. Jesus told them that the Spirit's arrival was for their good, since the Spirit was the One who would "prove the world to be in the wrong about sin and righteousness and judgment" (v. 8). Jesus then said to them,

> I have much more to say to you, more than you
> can now bear. But when he, the Spirit of truth,
> comes, he will guide you into all the truth. He

will not speak on his own; he will speak only
what he hears, and he will tell you what is yet to
come. (vv. 12–13)

If I had to net out the single most important reason I'm
devoted to evicting static from my life, it's that I desperately need
the guidance into all truth that Jesus says is mine in him. And the
truth is, so do you. When we tune in to God, we learn things from
his Spirit that we wouldn't have learned any other way. When we
tune in to him, things get revealed to us that we could never have
known otherwise.

When we tune in to him, we're filled with divine wisdom that
people in the natural realm would love to have. When we tune in
to him, we become a stabilizing force that can anchor those being
tossed about by the wind. It's only when we're living tuned in to
God that we experience life as it's meant to be lived. It's only when
we're living tuned in to God that we have anything useful to say.

TUNING IN | CHAPTER 2
Respond

1. What doubts do you harbor about God? That his grace is too good
to be true, perhaps? That his love has to be earned somehow? That
he would never speak to the likes of you? Or something else entirely?

2. What thoughts come to mind as you consider the idea that a
loving, gracious God is, in fact, speaking to you, and that the static
that is keeping you from hearing his voice is actually your doing
instead of his?

3. What type of static do you find causes the most interference in your life?

- Distraction: What people, responsibilities, dynamics, or desires tend to take your attention away from hearing God's voice?
- Stubborn independence: In what ways have you caused your life to run so smoothly that you've rendered God's intervention largely unnecessary—at least in your estimation?
- Disobedience: What requests has God made of you in the past that you have yet to fulfill? What effect do you suppose neglect of this type has on your ability to communicate clearly with him today?

Reflect

At the end of the chapter, I made this assertion:

> When we tune in to God, we learn things from his Spirit that we wouldn't have learned any other way. When we tune in to him, things get revealed to us that we could never have known otherwise. When we tune in to him, we're filled with divine wisdom that people in the natural realm would love to have. When we tune in to him, we become a stabilizing force that can anchor those being tossed about on the wind. It's only when

we're living tuned in to God that we experience life as it's meant to be lived. It's only when we're living tuned in to God that we have anything useful to say.

Do you buy these ideas? Why or why not?

Read On

Read the story in 1 Samuel 8 of the Israelites begging God for a king. In what ways can you relate to the idea that someone or something other than God can take better care of you than he can?

3

TUNED IN

Prayer is not asking. Prayer is putting oneself in the hands of God,
at His disposition, and listening to His
voice in the depth of our hearts.

—Mother Teresa

Several months ago I was heading into a lunch meeting at a local restaurant and ran into a guy I know through New Life. We caught up for a few minutes in the parking lot, enjoying easy conversation and a few laughs. I offered a handshake as we were departing, but instead of reaching for my hand, he said, "Hey, Brady, I need to mention one other thing to you."

He went on to tell me that two men who had been on staff at New Life but had accepted new roles in different churches a year or so prior were aggravated with me because they felt I'd dropped the ball in keeping in touch with them. This guy was a friend of theirs, and he had noticed that whenever he got together with them and my name or New Life Church came up, they both shut down. He wanted me to know so that I could do my part in patching up the relationships.

The update stuck with me through the day and bugged me every time it came to mind. I hated the thought of men with whom I'd worked—men I still considered buddies—thinking I was blowing them off. As the afternoon wore on, I found myself asking God with increased frequency what I should do.

With his Spirit leading, I did a quick examination of my heart. Was I frustrated with these guys for leaving our staff? I wasn't. While I'd hated to see them both go, I totally understood why they wanted to pursue new opportunities. Was I harboring some sort of ill will toward them that was going unaddressed? Not at all. These men were like brothers to me, even though our recent lack of proximity meant I didn't get to talk to them as much as I would have liked. Was I running so fast and furiously in my roles as husband, father, and leader that I was neglecting to connect with people I said I cared about? I didn't feel quite as confident about my answer to that one.

So I made a lunch appointment with the two men.

As soon as the three of us were sitting face-to-face across from one another, I jumped in. "Listen, I know you've both been aggravated with me," I said, "and the reason I wanted to get together was to tell you that I don't want any dissonance in our relationship. I don't want to aggravate you."

The air in the room shifted immediately. The tension that had been present was now gone. Before either of them could say anything, I continued: "Let me tell you how I feel about you two. I love you. I respect you. I admire you. And I want to continue being friends."

The next thirty minutes were pure gold. Before the meeting I'd asked God to give me words to say that would bless my friends and not curse them, that would draw them near rather than push them away. I asked God to help me actively listen and really hear what my friends had to say. I asked him to replace any tendencies toward selfishness or defensiveness with compassion, humility, and grace. Basically I wanted static-free airwaves that afternoon so that I could hear God clearly and not stick my foot in my mouth. And as I patiently listened while my two friends explained why they'd been feeling that I had marginalized them, my prayers were answered, three for three.

I left that meeting totally energized. My buddies and I had talked about the power of close proximity and about how intentional we'd need to be to stay in touch across the miles that now separated us. We talked about a few practical ways the three of us could avoid the relational drift that seems to occur naturally when one or both parties move away. And we talked about how good it felt to start fresh and move forward in unity. Our relationship wasn't just salvaged as a result of that meeting; it was made stronger than it had ever been.

That simple get-together showcases something I'm trying diligently to grasp these days, which is the first of the prophetic progression's four conversations: when I focus first on communicating with God—seeking his perspective, asking for his wisdom, slowing down to hear what he has to say—I have a reservoir from which to draw as I engage with the people I'm called to bless.

As I reflect on the situation with my two buddies now, I see that if I'd refused to solicit God's input, the meeting never would have occurred. I would have said nothing to them and just blown them off, or else I would have fired off an email using defensive language I'd probably have regretted later. I had a choice in the dilemma I faced with my two friends. I could choose preoccupation and posturing, which would have led me away from the others centeredness and unity that the way of Christ prizes, or I could choose to humbly engage. I chose the latter, even as the self-protective part of me threw a fit.

I chose intentional and unrushed conversation that centered on listening and loving well, because when life and death are the two choices—spiritual, relational, or otherwise—things go better when I choose life.

LESSONS FROM THE BULLY PULPIT

The reason I can boast about my conversational competence with my two pals is because of what I'm about to confess to you. While I was still floating on the success of that lunch meeting, during a Sunday-morning service a few weeks later, I openly berated one of our staff teams in front of our entire congregation, from right there onstage.

What happened was that I'd met with some of the audiovisual staff who run our church's production elements. They make sure the lights are doing what they're supposed to do, that the video screens have the right thing running at the right time, and that people in the auditorium can hear what is being said or sung from the stage—that type of thing. The reason I called the meeting was that there had been some issues during recent weekends, times when excellence was lacking and precision was nowhere to be found.

Microphones weren't being muted at the right times, PowerPoint slides were delayed or loaded with typos, camera angles weren't shifting quickly enough, and the net effect was a sloppy experience at best. I explained all of this to members of the team and then engaged them in a friendly dialogue about how to tighten up our practices. I left the meeting feeling great, but that feeling would fade about twenty minutes into the following Sunday's service.

Despite our agreement on all the ways we were going to sharpen things, during that service I noticed that each time I referenced a passage of Scripture or a key point in my talk, the slide that was on the screens positioned throughout the auditorium was not the proper one. I'd be explaining the second point in my sermon, for instance, but notice that the slide was still on the first point.

Or else I'd need to read aloud a swath of important Bible verses, but upon glancing at the screens to ensure the congregation was reading the same thing I was reading, I'd realize those verses weren't being projected. The delay wasn't just a few piddly seconds either; we're talking fifteen- or twenty-second delays. It was noticeable. I'd had enough.

Regretfully, instead of investing the nanosecond it would have taken to swallow my frustration and get through the balance of the service in an honorable fashion, there before God and a crowd seven thousand strong, I shouted toward the sound booth at the back of the room, "Hey! Keep up with me back there!" To make matters worse, I didn't have a smile on my face as I shouted. It wasn't an "Oh, those crazy kids. They must be dozing off during my sermons again—heh, heh, heh." No, it was "Hello, fools? Yes, I'm talking to you! If you'd like to keep your jobs, you'll keep up!"

It wasn't my finest moment.

Between the first and second services, I retreated to my office as usual, where I gathered myself and prepared to deliver my talk once more. Moments later Pam showed up. She never comes to my office between services; I knew this couldn't be good.

I greeted her and then asked, "What's up?" to which she asked, "Are you okay?"

I knew what "Are you okay?" meant. It meant "Clearly, you are *not* okay, given the bullying you did from the pulpit this morning."

I was bullied to within an inch of my life as a kid, the most pronounced memory centering on a group of high school boys tying a rope around my neck noose style, attaching the rope to the back of one of their cars, and then dragging me up a dirt hill until I was nearly unconscious.

I *hate* bullying.

And yet in that moment, while standing onstage, I became the very thing I hated.

"I'm frustrated" was all I managed to say to Pam, who then said, "Brady, your words were too strong."

If there was any silver lining to the situation, it's that immediately after Pam confronted me, my stiff heart turned elastic once more. I knew I'd been strong—too strong. I went in search of my tech team and apologized and then vowed to myself that I'd watch my words.

TWO STEPS FORWARD, ONE STEP BACK

If you've ever tried to learn a new language or take up violin or improve your golf game by changing your swing, you know that the early days of doing anything new will be a little rough. Your mind understands what your body is supposed to do, but your body is so unfamiliar with the new demands and movements that it gets repeatedly confused.

My son Abram was awarded his black belt in Tae Kwon Do last year, but he wasn't always so coordinated and swift. His first lessons were rudimentary at best—"Here's how you bow to the master." "Here's how you assume fight position." "Here's how you accomplish a simple kick."

But over time he developed confidence and skill until he reached black-belt status. Like any endeavor we eventually master, the place to begin is at the beginning. This goes for using our words well too. We think that because we've mastered the alphabet and basic grammar and the give-and-take of healthy conversational exchanges, we're good communicators. But if this were true, then why do so many "good communicators" say such stupid things? (I'm including myself here, as my bully-pulpit story clearly demonstrates.) The answer is what's at the heart of this book: there is a *soulish literacy* that must also be present if we're to steward our syllables well.

The first lesson in that curriculum is soliciting input from our holy God—not once but over and over again. In the same way that a novice basketball player has to practice positioning his elbow under the ball, keeping his knees slack until he fires, releasing the ball just before the top of his jump, and arching his shooting arm like a swan as the ball soars toward the goal, when we're just starting out on our journey toward wise communication, we have to submit to the rigors of training—"Here's how you subdue your self-absorption."

"Here's how you ask God for input." "Here's how you hear from heaven." "Here's how you say wise things." And so on.

This is anything but a linear process, as the back-to-back experiences I've already mentioned can attest. On one of those occasions, I handled the communiqué flawlessly, but on the other I crashed and burned. This is par for the course, I've found. Tuning in to God in the hope of learning to tame our tongues is a two-steps-forward-one-step-back kind of deal. We'll get it right and then get it horribly wrong, and then get it right and then wrong again.

At face value this may seem like bad news, but if you look deeper, you'll see it's not. Because while you and I will never communicate perfectly—every exchange, every single day—our wrongs will become less wrong as we learn. We'll start to naturally sink our shots.

The Bible says it this way: Jesus is the good shepherd, we as his children are his beloved sheep, and his sheep always listen for his voice (see John 10:27). The metaphor speaks to the training required, for the only way to have a sheep come when you call it is to train the sheep using repetition, shoulder scratches, and a ton of tasty feed.

Fail to train the sheep, and you'll have to rely on the services of a good sheepdog all the days of that sheep's life. Forceful herding will be your only option. I don't know about you, but I don't want God to "herd" me. I'd much rather enjoy the type of relationship with him that so many prophets described, where they communed with God, friend to friend, walking intimately, sharing life.

And so we sign up for rigorous training, asking God before, during, and after every conversation we have, *What are your thoughts on this, God? What are you up to here? What are you after in this person's life and mine? What can I say that would be in accordance with your will?*

In short, we get better at prayer.

ENROLLING IN THE SCHOOL OF PRAYER

If you've run in Christian circles for any amount of time, you've surely been told of the benefits of prayer. Prayer centers us and steadies us, it unburdens us and grounds us, it renews us and transforms us, it yields hopefulness and a sense of peace. And yet *still*, despite all the undeniable advantages we nod our heads in agreement with, most of us neglect to pray. I liken it to the way we regard the engines of our cars. We know they're important, that they ought to matter deeply to us, and yet if we're honest, we'd have to admit that we have no idea how they work.

If you're a gear guy (or gal) who knows the ins and outs of car engines, you could definitely teach me a thing or two. I wish I could be the one in the driveway with his head under the hood of his truck who actually knows what he's looking at. I wish I knew where the oil even goes, let alone how to change it, and yet to this day I don't.

I do know where the battery is, and I know how to charge that bad boy too. I know about the red-and-black cables—the positives, the negatives—and how not to die while jumping a car. But outside of that, I'm ignorant beyond belief. In fact, if my wife happened to come outside and find the hood of my truck up and me standing there nodding knowingly, as though I were actually going to *do* something under that hood, she would bust out laughing and say, "You have no idea what you're doing, Brady! I know you better than that."

That's exactly what she would say. And sadly, she would be right.

"Yep, Pam. Just sorting out the rattle I've been dealing with. Probably the flux capacitor or something, babe. Don't worry your pretty little self. This truck? It's in *real good hands.*"

Yeah, right. Maybe if pigs were flying and an ice storm were barreling through hell.

I bring up all this nonsense because I think that, to our endless detriment, we tend to approach the matter of prayer in the same way. The drumbeat of all of Scripture is that if we'll tune our lives to God's will, we will be wise and we will know peace, and that the process and practice of prayer is the way we gain access to that peace and wisdom, and that through prayer we can do some pretty cool things, such as move mountains and salvage the messes we've made of our lives. But what do we do when we come to prayer, to God's chosen method for moving heaven and earth? We regard it just like I regard the engine of my truck: *I know this thing ought to matter to me, but I can't for the life of me tell you why.*

Years ago I reread the account of Jesus on the cross and got to the part where Jesus was led out to be crucified. But he wasn't led out alone. "Two other men, both criminals, were also led out with him to be executed," Luke 23:32 says. "When they came to the place called the Skull, they crucified him there, along with the criminals—one on his right, the other on his left" (v. 33).

One of those criminals was a scoffer, his words dripping with sarcasm and spite: "Save yourself, Mr. Messiah. And while you're at it, save us too" (v. 39, paraphrased). Those in the crowd who shared this attitude spat at Jesus. They gambled for his few remaining garments. They offered him sips of sour wine. They mocked him with *faux* deference: "At last! We've found the King of the Jews!" But not everyone scoffed at God incarnate. Some chose to bear up under Jesus's pain. Instead of scoffing, they decided to sojourn, quietly holding vigil while their Messiah was killed.

The second criminal was numbered among this group. Shocked and horrified by the vicious turn of events Jesus was made to endure, he looked at the scoffer and asked, "Don't you fear God … since you are under the same sentence? We are punished justly, for we are getting what our deeds deserve. But this man has done nothing wrong" (vv. 40–41).

At the climactic moment in the story, that second criminal turned toward Jesus with humility and placed his life in the Savior's hands. "Jesus, *remember me when you come into your kingdom*," he said to Christ, to which Jesus replied, *"Truly I tell you, today you will be with me in paradise"* (vv. 42–43).

Basically Jesus told him, "The relief you're seeking, the peace from earthly pain, all the forgiveness and fortitude and future goodness you're after are yours, right here, right now."

The text says that moments after the exchange between the sojourner and Christ, darkness fell across the whole land, eclipsing even the sun's blazing rays. The curtain in the temple was torn down the middle, symbolizing that Christ's sacrifice was complete, and direct access to the heavenly Father was now officially granted to all. Then Jesus shouted, "Father, into your hands I commit my spirit" (v. 46). With those words, he breathed his last.

The thief on the cross who humbled himself before Christ reflected what Jesus had modeled all along: *reconciliation with God comes by choosing to place ourselves in his hands.* Our thoughts, our habits, our wishes, our whims, our wants—the sum of all we are and all we ever hope to be—handed over, willfully, to God.

The British Methodist minister Samuel Chadwick called prayer the "acid test of devotion"[1] in a believer's life, which I think is a reasonable way to describe it. Engaging with God in prayer is the one thing that shoves me out of rugged-independence mode and reminds me that "my life" is not my own at all. Prayer is what was happening when that contrite thief shifted his gaze toward Jesus and, with humility, put his life into Christ's hands.

For several years now, I've begun each day with morning prayer. The words I use tend to vary from day to day, even as the overarching themes stay the same. Most times I pray some version of these words:

> *Good morning, Father. Today, Lord, I ask you to set my eyes on your purposes, even at the exclusion of my own. Let me not look to the left or to the right but instead stay laser focused on your plan, setting you apart as Lord. Show me where you are leading me and give me the wisdom and energy to follow. Help me to make good decisions. Help me to use my words well. Help me to look and act like you today. Help me to be a giver of grace.*

It's not an earth-shattering prayer, by any means, but on the days when I really, really mean what I'm saying, those words are game changers for me. For its seemingly benign construction, the reason this prayer is so penetrating and challenging for me is that in order to let the words be activated in my life, I have to get honest with God. I have to acknowledge that the purposes of my often-wayward heart do not naturally run along the same lines as God's. I have to admit to him that I get distracted by the things of this world approximately 100 percent of the time.

I have to confess to him the self-focused, self-protective decisions I'll be prone to making that day unless his Spirit graciously intervenes. I have to remind him (and me as well) that I stick my foot in my mouth with astounding frequency, and that the only way I will say anything helpful or humble once I get up from my time with him and start interacting with humankind is for him to place wise words on my tongue. My morning prayer makes me remember that I don't look and act like God and like grace in my own strength, my own initiative, or my own will, and that blissfully, I'm not on my own that day.

During my morning prayer, God whispers to me, *Brady, you can't do better than the gifts I have in store for you as you choose to stay connected to me.*

Admittedly this connection is sometimes more difficult than it sounds to maintain. I'm thinking of a particular time when a man who was part of our fellowship at New Life approached me following a Sunday service to set me straight on the age of planet Earth. I had postulated partway through my sermon that the belief many of us have held that the earth is only six thousand years old might be errant, and "wouldn't it be interesting" if we were proved wrong. I knew full well the fleeting comment would ruffle the tail feathers of a certain percentage of our community, but what is church meant to be, if not a safe place to ask tough questions and work out the answers together?

Well, this man was having none of this "blasphemous talk," as he called it. He laid into me there at the altar, concluding his comments with the strong exhortation for me to be "ashamed" of myself, which is when I felt a tiny bit of rage bubbling up from the bottom of my gut. In the nanosecond it would have taken for that rage to find its way into words, I sensed the unmistakable presence of God instead. *Slow down, Brady,* he seemed to be saying. *Let self-control be your friend.*

I felt my face relax into a smile as the man stood there red faced, awaiting a response. I told God I didn't want to botch the exchange, that I wanted to go his way instead of mine. A moment later I stuck out my right hand and said to the New Lifer, "Listen, I come in peace. I'm a man of peace. Can we find a way to dialogue about this instead of treating it like a war to be won?"

"I just don't see how you can believe such garbage!" he boomed. "Especially given how clear the Bible is on this point."

He was no longer jabbing a finger toward my face as he spoke, though, so I counted that as progress. His words still carried an edge, but at least he'd stuffed his hands into his pants pockets now. I chose to see the subtle nonverbal as the equivalent of removing his arrows from the string of his bow and laying them across one another—a conciliatory move.

From there things improved further still. In the span of about five minutes, we'd swapped stories about who and what had influenced our beliefs along the way, eventually coming to the agreement that there are issues of core doctrine and then there are less-core distinctions we make along the way. And while we tend to feel very passionate about and protective of those less-core distinctions about our faith and heritage, they certainly don't need to be the reason we sever relational ties.

He half nodded, half shook his head, mulling over what I'd said, thinking maybe—*just maybe*—we could agree to disagree for now. "Let's talk again," he offered, to which I said cordially, "I'd like that. But how about a little less fire next time?"

He grinned, and then he said, "Hey, your LSU Tigers going to do anything this year?"

And that was that.

WHAT'S OUR GOAL, ANYWAY?

The exchange with the young-earth proponent forced me to reassess my goals as they relate to the conversations I have. When my goal is to assert my position at all costs, making sure I get to say my piece, things never go very well. But when I work to win intimacy with Jesus more than I work to win an argument with another person, I start looking like a modern-day prophet—one who calls on *all the resources of heaven* so that he can use his words to strengthen, encourage, and build others up.

We can practice prophetic communication right in the middle of any exchange, a topic we'll explore more in part 4 of this book. Whether the conversation is lighthearted or heated, weighty or benign, we can silently solicit help from heaven so that we know how to proceed with our words.

Any ideas here, Father? (That right there is a pretty good start. You'll recall that the psalmists always prayed this way.)

Help me, God!

I'm in a tight spot here, God!

Give me wisdom, God.

Make sense of this madness, please!

I'm better when I pray this way too—a better communicator, a better friend, a better follower of Jesus Christ.

When a man and a woman who are married and were once in love are no longer in love and thus no longer want to be married, there's a term for that. When they file their legal paperwork and begin the path toward divorce, what they cite is "irreconcilable differences." What this typically means is what drove the couple to part ways wasn't an extramarital affair, abuse, incurable insanity, or any real fault on either part. In fact, as they show up with separate lawyers to the appointed meeting place, they may even still love each other. The problem is, somewhere along the way they quit *liking* each other, and now they'd like to move on—separate and alone.

What took me some time to sort out after surrendering my life to the lordship of Christ during that drive home in August 1988 was that the initial reconciliation I was experiencing wasn't the only reconciliation I'd need to make. It's true that, just as the kinder of the two thieves on the cross realized, positional reconciliation with God can happen in an instant. *Future goodness! Here! And now!*

What's also true is that for those of us not being executed on a cross, following our initial profession of faith in Christ, a thousand more reconciliations will need to occur over the course of life. We get sideways with people with great frequency, don't we? Not just occasionally, here and there, but all the time. Such disconnects are never the will of God, which means that each time we encounter a conversational challenge, we need to surrender to his lordship all over again.

When I was stepping down from the platform that Sunday morning, and that man laid into me before so much as saying hello, my first inclination was to power up over him, telling him he had no right to speak to me that way. My second was to patronize him, refreshing his understanding of the counseling services our church offers people—*like him*—with anger issues.

What I *rarely* feel like being in the face of someone's rage is a person of peace, a person connected to God and therefore hitched to nonaggression and steadiness and joy. And yet that's exactly what God drew out of me that day when I turned to him instead of giving in to my own inclinations.

Then I remember the thief turned toward Jesus with humility and placed his life in the Savior's hands. "[And] Jesus answered him, 'Truly I tell you, today you will be with me in paradise'" (Luke 23:43).

Over and over again we have to do this if we plan to walk humbly with God.

Over and over again we need to tell God, "I'm the sheep, and you're the shepherd. I'm listening for your input. I'll do what you say."

When you and I choose to stay intimately connected to Christ—determined to hear from him, ready to serve his purposes whenever he calls—we get handed opportunities to convey truth to the people God loves. Yes, there are times when God shows up directly and communicates firsthand to his followers—in various places in the Bible his words came in a whisper, in a shout, in a burning bush, in a storm—but more often than not, God looks to ordinary people (and even an occasional donkey, as in Numbers 22:28) to deliver extraordinary truth. He looks to you and to me, even as he overlooks our inadequacies, and says, *You be the one to speak on my behalf. You go say what I'm asking you to say.*

This is the whole enchilada right here. What I'm about to tell you will change your life. When you press into the presence of your heavenly Father, you'll speak with pertinence, passion, and power. What you say will *matter*. What you say will *stick*. And what you say will call upon others to live well.

When we walk through our days with a *Speak, Lord* on our lips, leaning in to hear the whispers of heaven, longing to fulfill the wishes of God, God looks at us and says, *You'll never go hungry from this moment forward. You'll always be satisfied in me.*

TUNING IN | CHAPTER 3
Respond

1. In what ways can you relate to the idea that making progress in any facet of life isn't always linear?

2. As it relates to how you use your words, how would you describe the gains you've made over the years? What relational setbacks have you experienced?

3. How does the idea sit with you that prayer is nothing more than putting yourself in the hands of God? What assumptions, training, or firsthand experiences inform your thoughts?

4. What words would your own morning prayer include, or if you already have a morning prayer, how might it change for the positive?

Reflect

What might be different about your ability to hear from God if you began each day with a morning prayer (if that is not already part of your current routine)? Consider giving it a try this week.

Read On

Read the full account of Jesus's death, burial, and resurrection found in Luke 23. What emotions do you suppose Jesus was feeling as the criminal on the cross beside him asked Jesus to remember him?

PART TWO

THE CONVERSATION
BETWEEN YOU
AND YOURSELF

4

WHICH VOICE WINS?

Our decisions, our relationships, and our preferences in large
part stem from what we say to ourselves about ourselves.
—Ruth Graham, *In Every Pew Sits a Broken Heart*

During my growing-up years, money was tight—at times, *really*
tight, as in "Don't bother asking about what's for dinner, because
the bare cupboard will just laugh in your face" tight. Interestingly,
I didn't really know that my family was poor. Most of the people
living in our neck of the Louisiana woods were struggling to get
by, so the fact that we were struggling to get by meant we were part
of the in crowd.

But that sense of inclusion would soon fade.

After I completed high school and then college—a first in my
family—and then got a job and another job after that, I started
noticing that people around me weren't struggling nearly as much.
They always had food to eat, for instance. Not only that, but they
also drove nice cars and wore nice clothes and actually took things
called vacations from time to time.

The more I advanced in life, the more frequently I found
myself in the presence of people who were downright rich. And

each time I encountered "rich," I was tempted to buy in to the notion that I was poor—or more specifically, that I was poor, I'd always been poor, and poor was all I'd ever be. It was a terrible stigma, the sheer force of which took me decades to overcome.

THE AGREEMENTS WE MAKE

My buddy John Eldredge and I were hanging out one afternoon a while back when he recounted a conversation he'd had earlier that day with his wife, Stasi. John was leaving for a meeting he wasn't looking forward to, and on his way out of the house, he said, "Well, off I go. This meeting is just going to *suck*."

Stasi, exasperated, replied, "John. Seriously. Now you've named it 'The Meeting That Is Going to Suck,' so guess what is going to be true of the meeting? *It's going to suck*."

Realizing that Stasi was right as usual, John sighed.

I absolutely love that conversation. I love it because this is *John Eldredge* we're talking about, the guy who literally wrote the book on the perils of making agreements with negative thoughts, words, beliefs, and ideas. The fact that even *he* doesn't bat a thousand somehow encourages my soul.

Actually, John has written several books on the perils of making negative agreements, but the one that comes to mind right now is *Walking with God*. In the scene I'm thinking about, John was facing a bout of writer's block, which happens from time to time to everyone who tries to put pen to paper. But this bout was "oppressive," John said. Something about it felt intense. To make matters worse, on the heels of acknowledging the block—*I'm just having an off morning*—he sensed himself stepping toward a secondary assessment, an "agreement," if you will, with a negative thought. It went like this: *I'm just having an off morning.... I guess I'm just not going to get anything done today.*[1]

Do you see how subtle that leap was? He used a relatively benign situation—being momentarily stuck in the task of putting together a paragraph—as fuel for declaring doom over his entire workday.

It's not just John who does this type of thing; you and I are guilty of it too. Making negative agreements is the default behavior for *all* of us, the undertow forever threatening to take us down and keep us there until we drown. This idea is what was at the center of my temptation to believe that impoverishment was my destiny and that scarcity would define my days. Years later it would be the reason I nearly caved under the weight of believing I wasn't just poor; I was a *bona-fide* idiot as well.

When I was twenty-three years old, I transitioned from the business world into ministry and took a job at a private Christian school that was located on the same campus as the church that had started it. I was to be the school's campus pastor, as well as a high school teacher and basketball coach.

The school's team was made up of a group of guys who were white, short, slow, and just plain bad, but because I wanted to be near the sport, and because I was eager to please the senior pastor who also served as the school's principal and was a man I deeply respected and admired, I agreed to coach the team. I quickly realized that even my lone seven footer couldn't dunk the ball, which was a foretaste of the awfulness to come.

During a midseason game against our crosstown rival, my key player (I'm being generous here), who was frustrated by the whupping our team was getting out on the court, started copping an attitude. I was young and impulsive, and so instead of choosing to let him finish the game and effectively give us our best shot at a comeback, I benched him and gave him the cold shoulder the rest of the night. I should have punished him privately the next day by making him run wind sprints or something, but I didn't. I humiliated him in front of his teammates, the players' families, and about two hundred fans watching from the bleachers with jaws agape.

Of course our team got pummeled that night, and after the game, when the guys had headed for the locker room to shower and change clothes, the principal approached me to register his discontent. I knew he would be disappointed with the loss, having been a former sports star himself years before, but the words he chose to say to me equated to vehicular homicide of the heart. I didn't see the oncoming collision, recklessness that would level me for years to come.

He stood within inches of my nose and said, "Brady, you looked stupid out there tonight. What were you thinking benching him? Stupid! What a stupid thing to do." With that he stormed off in a huff.

As I say, this man was my pastor. My boss. In some ways, even my friend. His opinion carried great weight, and his opinion was that I was a fool. The wound in my heart was the size of Texas. *Was I, in fact, stupid?* My parents had never told me I was stupid. And my friends, while they may have suspected it, surely never used that term. My pastor's reckless words formed a dagger in my heart that wedged its way deeper with each passing day.

The following week my pastor apologized, but in my heart, the damage had been done. It would take me a full fifteen years to recover from his penetrating comments, and even after that, the wound was tender still. I was poor *and* I was stupid. I knew these two things to be true. Negative agreements tend to run deep like that, redefining the person we believe we are.

But I know I'm not alone in this, based on the stories I hear every week.

An entrepreneur who launched two profitable companies in twelve months' time *still* refuses to believe he's successful, because he continues to hear the words of his father all those years ago: "You're a loser. I'm sorry you're my son."

A teenage girl, replaying her mother's bitter words—"I'm through with you!"—cycles through one sexual encounter after another in hopes of finding someone who will stick around.

A forty-something woman who is in shape and just completed a triathlon *still* can't make peace with her body because of that immature boy in her fifth-grade class who greeted her with "Hi, fatso!" day after day.

A young man can't seem to find motivation to get off the couch, get a job, and get out of his parents' basement. His inaction, in effect, answers his folks' long-standing question: "Why can't you be more like your (brilliant, talented, and accomplished) brother?"

An adolescent exhibits reprehensible behavior at school and then is told he "should be ashamed" of himself. A vicious, self-fulfilling cycle of shame followed on the heels of that scolding. (When I heard this particular story from the student's parent, I nodded my head in recognition. When I was a kid, it was common for adults in our community to say these exact words to misbehaving children. They were probably just saying what their own parents had said to them, but talk about a fast path to a damaged self-concept: "*You should be ashamed of yourself*"? We can do better than this.)

Start paying attention to your self-talk on a given day, and you'll probably find a few negative agreements lurking around your life too—often echoing words spoken to you in the past. You have a restless night of sleep and get out of bed mumbling, "It's going to be a long day." Your middle schooler drops the midbreakfast grenade that he forgot about a project that's due today, and you hear yourself say with exasperation, "You're *never* going to be on top of your schoolwork, are you?"

Your boss texts you a request to see you "as soon as you get to the office," and even before you ask for clarification on the nature of the meeting, you expect the worst. Construction makes your commute sluggish, to which you say, "Looks like nothing is going to go right today." Your engine light comes on, to which you say, "Of course. There goes another few hundred bucks." Your cell phone lights up with a call from your wife, bringing to mind the tense (and unresolved) disagreement about money the two of you had last night. Before you take the call, a thought races through your consciousness: *We're always going to fight this fight.* You get off the phone as you pull into work, which is when you realize that you completely spaced a board presentation you were scheduled to make this afternoon. You think, *I'm just as delinquent as my preteen son! No wonder he is such a flake.*

On and on it goes, and all before 9:00 a.m. A few brief mental cycles into your day, and you've decided you're an exhausted and ill-prepared imbecile who is a sorry excuse for a parent, a clear failure as a spouse, and based on upcoming, unplanned expenses, soon to be broke.

Now, what effect do you suppose agreements such as these have on a person's desire or ability to engage in healthy, life-giving communication with another human being? It can't be a positive one. We can't give what we don't have, and when our energies are consumed with self-flagellation, we fall short in our efforts to help others thrive.

"DO I GET A VOTE TOO?"

There's another voice vying for our attention the entire time the evil whispers of self-reproach are seducing us, and that voice belongs to God. When I look back on the strains of negative self-talk that have arrested my progress along the way, I see how all-consuming those downward spirals were. It didn't matter which aspect of life I was evaluating, *everything* seemed broken and wrong. In my healthier moments, I can see that God was there all along, beckoning me back to sanity, even as I ignored his still, small voice and continued heading south. Actually, on a few occasions I ignored his strong, booming voice too—self-hatred can get pretty loud.

I envision God watching us as we get reeled in—hook, line, soul-level sinker—to the lies that we're useless or hopeless or stupid or poor, and as he watches, he's thinking, *Wait. Do I get a vote here at all?* Because if he did—if we would just let *him* weigh in on our worth—we would learn that we are precious and priceless and pure. Remember, when God commended his Son, Jesus had yet to perform a single miracle or woo even one crowd his way. After

John the Baptist submerged him in the water of the Jordan River, God the Father announced from heaven, "You are my Son, whom I love; with you I am well pleased" (Luke 3:22).

For many people—maybe even you?—this idea of acceptance that is granted *irrespective of* performance just doesn't compute. We live in such a pedigreed society that at every turn we're left feeling as if we're anything but enough. When we're in high school, assuming we make it that far, well-meaning friends and family members want to know where we're going to college. Halfway through our freshman year in college, they want to know what we're studying—what we'll "be" when we graduate.

When graduation day comes, we're expected to land a job somewhere notable, or at least secure a promising internship. From there the questions only persist about where we'll live, when we'll get married, when that first baby will arrive, when the next baby will come, and on and on it goes. Throughout this sequence, there is a constant assessment of what we're driving, what we're wearing, where we're going, and how our friendship circles are filling out.

For every single person I know, at least in their own minds, they fail the test. They're not doing enough right things. They're not seen at enough right places. They're not wearing enough right clothes. Any way they slice it, they're not enough, which only adds rich soil, water, and sunshine to the self-recriminatory seeds that were planted in their minds and hearts years or decades ago. Those criminal kernels grow and grow and grow, until at last they overtake every positive plant in their lives. What happened? I'll tell you what happened: *they didn't give God a vote.*

HE IS WELL PLEASED WITH YOU

During those same years when I was ignorant of the fact that my family wasn't exactly well off, even though I didn't have access to a wealth of material resources, I had access to *vast* storehouses of confidence and encouragement courtesy of my dad. Nearly every morning, just before he headed off to his blue-collar job at the poultry plant, he'd lay his hands on my shoulders and say, "Brady, I love you and I'm proud of you. You are smart, Son. And you can do anything you want in life."

Have you seen the movie *The Help*? In the same way that the character Aibileen Clark transformed the heart of her neglected young charge, Mae Mobley Leefolt, by telling her over and over, "You is kind. You is smart. You is important,"[2] my father equipped me with an overcomer's mind-set by speaking words of life and truth over me. In the decades to follow, I would face all the usual challenges life tends to dole out—trouble in school, breakdowns in relationships, shattered dreams, and more—and while I would momentarily cave in to those disappointments, over time I'd pop back up, thanks to an inner script that went something like this: "Yeah, this is a setback, but I'm going to be okay. I'm loved. I'm valued. I've got a good head on my shoulders and will figure this thing out."

I *wasn't* an impoverished person. I had the greatest resource a person could know: a father's deep and abiding love. Both sets of messages vied for my attention—"You are pitiful, Brady. You're poor and destined to fail" on one hand, and on the other, "You have every resource you need, Brady, for life and joy and success." And while I couldn't control their demanding pleas, I could choose with the decisiveness of a traffic cop managing a busy intersection which message to wave on through.

As a quick aside, it would take years and years for me to discover that my dad wasn't being entirely truthful with his well-meaning words of encouragement. Yes, it was true that he loved me. And yes, I would prove to be relatively smart. But the part about my being anything I wanted to be in life? That was total bunk. I know this now—now that I'm not an astronaut, a superhero, or the starting quarterback for the Dallas Cowboys, all roles I decidedly wanted back when I was a little kid. Still, my dad believed I *could* be any of those things, and for that, I loved the man.

What my dad did for me by giving me his stamp of approval—regardless of what I had or had not done, what I would or would not do in future days—set me up for success in terms of receiving God's acceptance. I tell dads all the time that they have a unique role to play in the lives of their children: to teach them by their father's words and actions how to respond to a loving God.

When an earthly father relates well with his kids, those kids have a much easier time relating well with their heavenly Father. This was certainly the case for me. My dad hinged his affinity for me not on anything I had said or done but on his own laudable qualities—namely, his maturity, his selflessness, his kindness, and his grace. This is exactly what God does with us.

Think back with me on the covenant God made with Abram in Genesis 17. He told Abram, who was already pretty much ancient by then, that he would be Abraham, the "father of many nations"—which had to make the old man laugh.

Go from your country, your people and your
father's household to the land I will show you.

I will make you into a great nation,
	and I will bless you;
I will make your name great,
	and you will be a blessing.
I will bless those who bless you,
	and whoever curses you I will curse;
and all peoples on earth
	will be blessed through you. (Gen. 12:1–3)

Now, typically, a contract is made between two parties and
is conditional in nature, meaning that both parties agree to do
their side of the deal, and if either party fails to do so, the contract is rendered null and void. But God is a maker of covenants,
not contracts. And while contracts can be broken, covenants are
permanent. God's covenant with Abraham was unconditional. It
was unilateral. It was God's alone to uphold. God made promises
to Abraham that required nothing of Abraham for them to come
to pass.

Genesis 15 says that "when the sun had set and darkness had
fallen, a smoking firepot with a blazing torch appeared and passed
between the pieces" (v. 17). That "blazing torch" symbolized the
presence of God, and the "pieces" refer to the halves of sacrificial
animals that had been laid down. The fact that only God walked
between those halves meant that only God was responsible for
keeping the promise. He was prepared to fulfill *both* halves of the

covenant—his *and* Abraham's. God was going to provide the bless-ing for the simple fact that Abraham was one of God's own. God is still in that business today.

When you and I keep returning to God, keep inviting him to speak into our lives, keep relishing his power and presence and provision, we tap into the blessings he promised to send to the earth through Abraham. We suddenly have access to what is prom-ised in various passages throughout Scripture. God will …

- free us (Ps. 118:5),
- plant us like trees by streams of water (1:3),
- bestow good things on us (31:19),
- promote us (75:6–7),
- protect us (41:1–2),
- deliver us (50:15),
- build us up (Jer. 24:6),
- keep us alive (Ps. 33:18–19), and
- pour out so much blessing that we will not have room enough for it (Mal. 3:10).

He does these things not because of any effort on our part but because this is who he is. When we encounter God, in other words, we can't help but encounter goodness and grace. In the same way that all I had to do to receive words of affirmation from my dad was to simply turn toward him and open my ears, all you and I must do to learn that God is well pleased with us is to point our feet in his direction and tune in.

SELF-TALK THAT IS TUNED IN TO GOD

I want to return to the scenario of the negative-self-talk morning, the one where you find yourself waking after a restless night saying, *It's going to be a long day*. What if instead of indulging gloom-and-doom tendencies, you were to say to yourself, *I've had better nights of sleep, but it's a new day, and I'm grateful for it. I have everything I need for life and godliness this day. Let's see what unfolds?*

I'm guessing things would go better for you.

I know they go better for me when I do that.

When we make a habit of communicating with God, we start believing that what he says about us is true. When we don't, we allow the other, louder voices to capture our attention and frame the course of our days.

I distinctly recall when my kids were twelve and ten that parents of teenagers would eye me pityingly and say, "Hope you're ready for what's coming, Brady. The teen years are *tough*." Once Abram and Callie were *bona-fide* teenagers, new acquaintances—also parents of teens—would discover the ages of my kids and the naysaying would escalate: "It's like aliens come down and inhabit them, right? Like, what happened to my sweet, loving kids? All of a sudden they're selfish, entitled brats who just want money! I bet you know just what I mean!"

I never really understood this tendency to declare awfulness over a seven-year-long period of time. That's a long time to eat the bitter fruit of negative self-talk, don't you think?

Instead, as my children entered their teenage years, I meditated on thoughts like these:

This is going to be our best era yet. Pam and I are going to love parenting teenagers. Abram and Callie are smart and funny, and our family is going to have an awesome time while they're teens. Whatever challenges we face as we parent teens, we will overcome together, and with love on our side.

Today Abram and Callie are seventeen and fifteen, respectively, and proof positive that experience flows from expectation. If we expect awfulness from life and loved ones, awfulness shows up every time, but if we expect greatness, then greatness tends to emerge instead.

So far the teen years have been great.

Here's another success story I can share. For a handful of years now, a group of leaders from New Life's staff and I have hosted newcomers to our church on Wednesday nights in a forum called New Life Next. It's an opportunity for guests to hear about our vision and mission, our operating values and community involvements, and ministry initiatives that might be relevant to them. Following a few brief presentations from various department heads, a block of time is set aside for a Q and A, where guests can ask about anything from the role of the Nicene Creed in our belief system (it's weighty) to the quality of the coffee served in our little café (it's slightly above average, at best).

Prior to the real meat of the discussion, I always kick off the evening with a fifteen-minute general overview of our church's founding and history. Our church received an abundance of international press in 2006 and 2007 from the scandalous departure of our founding pastor and the fatal shootings that occurred on our campus thirteen months later. Initially, because I didn't want guests to think I was trying to hide anything, I felt obliged to acknowledge both. And so I would.

Each Wednesday night, I stood in front of two or three hundred men and women, and with great soberness I discussed that difficult duo of events. The entire time I'd be speaking, my inner dialogue would go something like this: *No other church has suffered a scandal and a shooting like we have. These people are never going to come back after they hear what we've been through. I'm sure they don't feel safe here. They'll probably sneak out of this session before it's over, given how repulsed they already are with us.*

It never occurred to me that my self-talk might have had it wrong.

Several weeks into this practice, I couldn't help but notice an interesting trend. Almost without exception, my explanation of the scandal and the shooting was met with whispered side conversations held right then, during my talk. Later, during the Q-and-A session, those same people who had been whispering would raise their hands and ask questions such as, "There was a *shooting* here? I had no idea ..."

The challenges our church walked through had so marked us that I couldn't for the life of me understand how *anyone* didn't know what we'd endured—and yet they didn't. Colorado Springs is a highly transient town because of the myriad military installations we boast, and people from other parts of the country and the world had somehow missed a few weeks of pertinent news reports—at least, pertinent in the life of our church. So I began to adjust my remarks.

It was still important to me to be forthright, but I decided I could achieve that goal in a different way. Instead of dampening the entire session with explicit explanations of the tragic events, when it came time to walk through our history, I began saying, "We've endured deep heartache as a church, and we've also known great victory, and as we get to know you and you get to know us, you'll come to understand the significance of both …"

With satisfaction I then moved on to discussing the powerful things God was doing in our midst. There was no need to trumpet the tragedy, I determined, when that tragedy didn't define us as a church. Yes, the events had rocked us, and yes, they feel fresh in our memories still today, but to give the ashes greater weight than the beauty God created from them is to totally neglect the long view.

Reining in my doomsday thoughts and giving wings to more optimistic self-talk helped me change the tenor of those get-togethers for the better: *We should be a used-car lot given everything we walked through, but look at all that God is doing here! Who wouldn't want to be part of this church?* The impact of positive self-talk is evidenced each Wednesday night as hundreds of newcomers link arms with our church.

I could keep going with examples of how God is reforming my self-talk for the better—both in my heart and in the words I speak as a result—and yet, equally as true, I could share time after time when I caved in yet again to making negative agreements. In the next chapter, I'd like to explore the reasons why insecurity like this is so difficult to extract from our lives.

TUNING IN | CHAPTER 4
Respond

1. What do your typical self-talk themes reveal about your views on God and on yourself? (If you've never stopped to assess your self-talk before, here's a good question to start with: "What are the eight to ten most wonderful things about me, and what are the eight to ten things I desperately wish I could change?" Once you make your lists, see which side of the ledger you tend to live from most days, the positive or the negative.)

2. How does the idea that God is well pleased with you mesh with your understanding of who he is and who you are?

3. Which of the truths presented in this chapter do you wish you believed more wholeheartedly and lived from more frequently? Circle all that apply:

- God loves you.
- God will honor you.
- God will promote you.
- God will protect you.
- God will deliver you.
- God will build you up.
- God will keep you alive.
- God will richly bless you.
- God will give you goodness and grace.

Reflect

Based on your selection(s) above, meditate for a few minutes on what you think would change for you if you embraced each of these truths more completely.

Read On

Review Luke 3:21–22 in your Bible and imagine God speaking those same words over you today.

5
INSIDIOUS INSECURITY

*We're going to have to let truth scream louder to
our souls than the lies that have infected us.*
—Beth Moore, *So Long, Insecurity*

Despite the wins I've enjoyed over insecurity along the way, they
have proved to be mere battles in a long-standing war, not the
ultimate victory. My dad's unconditional love helped me make
continual progress in believing Jesus's claims that I am seen and
accepted and loved, but I had to learn the hard way that no matter
how many times I ran it out of town, insecurity wouldn't stay gone
for long.

In the same way black mold can get into the joints and mar-
row of a home, making it almost impossible to detect and expel,
insecurity seeps into self-talk's crevices, down deep where bugs
can't even go. To eliminate it forever, you have to take self-talk
down to its studs.

That's my goal with this chapter, to expose the foundation on
which insecurity is built.

SURE SIGNS OF INSECURITY

Being a student of insecurity throughout various seasons of my life has afforded me almost expert status on the subject, a distinction I certainly don't want. Still, there have been times when the depth of knowledge has come in handy, such as when God prompted me to preach on the topic of breaking free from insecurity's trap. *I can do that*, I told God in response, my confidence born of the realization that I'd essentially been preparing for that sermon for the entirety of my adult life.

Specifically I've noticed three hallmarks of insecurity whenever I've fallen into the clutches of believing I wasn't enough. I trust you'll find them useful too.

Sign No. 1: You Feel Inadequate

The most obvious indicator of insecurity is a prevailing sense of inadequacy. We feel inadequate when we tell ourselves we're inadequate, and the undeniable language of inadequacy seems to always be on our lips. It can slip through in fleeting comments, but listen closely and you'll pick it up.

It's the mom who laughs and says to her daughter, "Oh, honey, you'll be fine in life, as long as you're not like me." It's the man, age fifty, in a dead-end job, who says, "I should be doing better by this stage in life, shouldn't I?" It's the young person wishing for wisdom and the old one dying for youth. It's the pale person wishing for bronzed beauty, and the tan one despising sun-wrinkled skin. It's the structured person wishing for free spiritedness, and the spontaneous one pushing for some sort of routine. It's the food addict hoping to be thin someday, and the waif craving a five-course meal. It's the at-home parent eyeing those with exciting lives, and the excited person yearning for the peace of a day at home.

No matter who you are, what you have, where you've been, where you're going, what you look like, what you *are* like, or whom you know, it's likely you've felt inadequate at some point—wishing to be or do or have something else. If you tend to manifest any sign of insecurity, it will start to show up in your self-talk in comparison's ugly terms: "I'm not as strong as he is." Or "I'm not as successful as she is." Or "I'm not as put together as she is." Or "I'm not as articulate as he is." In fact, insecurity can take any number of forms:

- "My beard doesn't look as full."
- "My cooking doesn't taste as good."
- "My voice doesn't sound as smooth."
- "My shoes aren't nearly as cool."
- "My résumé doesn't read as well."
- "My house isn't worth as much."
- "My kids aren't doing as well."
- "My car isn't even close to that clean."
- "My tweets aren't as witty."
- "My online posts aren't as wise."
- "My words aren't as winsome."
- "And where are the bags underneath their eyes?"

On and on our comparisons go; where they will stop, nobody knows. If you're one who is suffocating underneath a shroud of inadequacy, then you know I'm not overstating things here. There are never any winners in the comparison game, just a jumbled heap of those who beat their heads on the brick wall of covetousness and let the joy of living get sucked out of them in the process. You can imagine how jolting it was for me to nearly land myself in that heap—and as recently as eight years ago.

The year was 2007 and I was at a crossroad. I hadn't yet accepted the lead role at New Life; in fact, the search committee had only just presented the invitation to me, which is what was throwing me for a loop. Until that point in time, I had been living in the Bible Belt—a region loosely encompassing the south-central and southeastern portions of the United States—where church attendance is higher and suspicions regarding megachurch pastors are lower.

In the Bible Belt I could more easily distract people from the fact that I have no Bible degree, no formal teacher or preacher training, and have never spent a single hour in a seminary classroom. But here in Colorado, which is where the search committee (and perhaps also my new job) was located, cynicism toward preachers reigns supreme. I just knew that if I said yes to the role, I'd spend every day waiting to be found out.

In an attempt to allay my fears, the head of the search committee said that his group had unanimously agreed that I was the perfect fit for the church, after which I protested and squirmed. I felt sure they'd gotten candidates' names mixed up. They didn't want me. They couldn't want me. I was unqualified and undereducated. (Oh, and while I'm at it: poor and stupid, don't forget.) My self-talk was in the tank—me, the secure, steady one they were calling on to lead a church of thousands.

In the brief span of time between the day that phone call came in and the day I told the search committee I'd love to serve as New Life's senior pastor, God penetrated my fortified walls of insecurity—*I'm the wrong guy. They don't want me. I'll never succeed in this endeavor. Because of these things, I won't even try.* He sent a clear message from his heart to mine. *I've called you to this role,* he all but whispered, *and I will make sure you prevail.*

This line of thinking went against my better judgment: How could someone with my laughable background do something as preposterous as *prevail?* I knew better than to buy into these lies. I knew that for the follower of Christ, what God says ultimately goes—and yet *knowing* something is far different from actually *acting* in accordance with that knowledge. It would be a long, hard road ahead for me, but it ultimately led to a beautiful place. For the realization that eventually unfolded was that the emphasis of God's promise wasn't on my prevailing; it was on God, who would bring that prevailing to pass. *I will make sure you prevail,* he had told me. He was the One I needed to trust.

Sign No. 2: You Feel Overlooked

An odd paradox is that even when we're feeling inadequate—and are whiling away our time comparing ourselves with everyone else (and losing at the game every stinking time)—there exists simultaneously in us a sense of sheer terror that our greatness is being overlooked. *How can this be?* you ask. I offer a one-word answer: *childishness.*

During my first days as a pastor, I had an insatiable need for people to tell me that I was called into ministry, that I was *good* at ministry, and that I was a special addition to the church's staff.

(Mind you, God had already confirmed in my heart that I was called to minister in his name. He told me he would guide me and pretty much guaranteed my success, as long as I stayed close to him.) But as soon as a few affirming comments came my way, I developed an appetite for more props. I started tilting conversations toward my performance in hopes of roping some attaboys … and broadcasting for anyone within earshot how desperately insecure I was.

I would have done well back then to meditate on the words of Proverbs 27:2: "Let someone else praise you, and not your own mouth; an outsider, and not your own lips." Since then I've come to understand that the reason I was left hungry for affirmation is that I was beating everyone else to the punch. I became a pro at self-promotion, which left little tolerance for much more of my greatness to be aired. I cringe when I revisit the truth of who I was, but in a section on minding one's self-talk, I'll simply say that I, for one, am grateful for the opportunity to grow and move on.

You and I need words of encouragement from time to time. In fact, speaking affirmation to others is one of the laudable practices we'll explore in part 4 of this book. I'm not suggesting that we reject others' kindness; I'm just saying we don't need to go trolling for it. God is the giver of all good gifts, including our special abilities, talents, propensities, and skills. We're engineered for greatness, and he is committed to using that greatness for good.

Sign No. 3: You Feel Threatened

Nobody wants to feel insecure. We want to feel sturdy and steady, safe and secure, unmovable, unshakable, and strong. We don't want to indulge negative agreements. The fact is, whenever insecurity trips our fight-or-flight mechanisms, our personal defense systems go into full alert, and we don't know what else to do. This is the first and most classic sign of insecurity, which is that we feel threatened by somebody, somewhere. Think King Saul in the presence of up-and-coming King David from days of old.

In 1 Samuel 18, we learn that David had just slain Goliath and was now rising to fame as a national hero. He had proved that he was skilled, we know that he was experienced, and the text says that whatever Saul sent David to do, the young man did it so successfully that he was quickly promoted through the ranks. David's reputation was growing rapidly throughout the nation of Israel.

As Saul's army was en route home from their defeat over the monstrous Philistine, the townswomen greeted them, flooding the streets in joyous song. They were dancing and playing tambourines while cheering, "Saul has slain his thousands, and David his tens of thousands" (v. 7). This arrested Saul in a flash. *Wait*, he thought, *isn't this festive occasion in my honor? Aren't these people here to celebrate me? They're crediting that pipsqueak with more victories than I've netted? How easily swayed can they be?*

Saul found the refrain galling. At that moment he determined in his heart to take David down.

The Bible confirms that Saul was a strong leader. He was capable, anointed, an A student in the gifted-and-talented classes of his day. And yet as soon as Saul's protégé showed signs of promise, Saul's inner voice went the hate-speech route. *David is going to usurp my authority*, Saul must have thought. *He's going to steal my thunder and win my crowd.* Saul couldn't stand for this, could he? No, David's influence must be dismantled—*fast.*

Hell bent on removing the threat to his own sure success, Saul spent the next eight years hunting down David all across Israel and the surrounding lands. The plan had been hatched in that split second when Saul's pride was threatened—*"Saul has slain his thousands, and David his tens of thousands!"* Despite all the good David was doing, Saul focused on banishing him instead of blessing him. In so doing, Saul morphed into the textbook definition of *insecure*—unstable, uncertain, unsure, and unsound. *Nobody* would treat Saul this way and live to tell about it! Not on his watch, anyway.

Now, by way of comparison, consider how Jesus responded to Pontius Pilate when he faced feeling threatened, vulnerable, and exposed. In John 19, just before Jesus was led away to his crucifixion, Pilate looked at him incredulously and said, "Do you refuse to speak to me? … Don't you realize I have power either to free you or to crucify you?" (v. 10), to which Jesus replied, "You would have no power over me if it were not given to you from above" (v. 11).

Ah. Touché! Jesus had a point we shouldn't miss. You see, the reason God doesn't want insecurity to dwell in our hearts is because insecurity never dwelled in Jesus's heart. And if we want the spirit of Jesus to live inside us, then we have to be willing to bid the spirit of insecurity farewell. Why? Because Jesus will not room with a spirit of insecurity—whenever he shows up, insecurity has to go.

Listen, the hatefulness that bubbles up in the attitude, articulations, and actions of one who resides in a threatened, high-alert state runs totally contrary to the way of Christ. Rather than hating the people who tried to threaten him, Jesus *loved them all the way to his own crucifixion*, an example that shows us it's possible to trust God for our future even when those around us are upsetting our way of life. The Bible says that instead of overreacting to others' insults, persecution, false accusations, or grave threats, Jesus "entrusted himself to him who judges justly" (1 Pet. 2:23). In other words, we don't have to orchestrate the win for ourselves. God's got it under control.

God sees our predicament, he cares about our stress, and he is committed to our making it to the other side alive. The Scriptures say that God "delights in every detail of [his people's] lives" (Ps. 37:23 NLT)—something we have a hard time believing, especially when it feels as if life has us in a headlock. But there the words stand, a clear promise for all to read.

We can regulate our breathing, let our shoulders fall, and rest assured that God has already put into place a mitigation plan for every threat we will face. When we give God our weakness, he will make us strong (see 2 Cor. 12:10) and enable us to overcome *anything* that threatens to overcome us. Those words have been a lifeline for me, especially as they relate to my health. Let me explain.

Over the past three or four generations, all the men in my family—fathers, uncles, grandfathers—have died either of massive heart attacks or from cancer, and always before eighty years of age. My grandfathers are dead. All of my uncles are dead. My own dad passed away at age sixty-three. As I write this, I'm forty-nine, and I already have a pacemaker in my chest. The math doesn't bode well for me.

As it relates to issues of health, you can deduce how my self-talk goes. At Thanksgiving there will be delicious food on the table, beloved family members in every corner of the house, football on

TV, and a nice chill in the air outside. And out of nowhere, despite my charming surroundings, I'll think, *What if I only have fourteen of these left to enjoy?* That was last Thanksgiving. This Thanksgiving, I might have only thirteen left.

If I die at age sixty-three, just as my dad did, Abram will be thirty-one and Callie will be twenty-nine. (I won't tell you how old Pam will be, because I prefer not to sleep on the couch.) Between now and then, that will mean thirteen more Christmases, thirteen Easters, thirteen more summer vacations. Thirteen more years, and that's it. I don't want thirteen more to be "it." I don't even want to think about "it." And yet from time to time, I do. I do, and then I freak out, and then I try to catch my breath but can't.

Here is what helps me on those days. Eventually I come back around to believing God, to believing what he says about the future and the hope I have in him. That he will provide for me. That he has good plans for me. As an aside, many famous missionaries have quoted the words of George Whitfield: "We are immortal till our work [on earth] is done"[1]—a very Calvinistic view, to be sure.

"Nothing bad can happen to me unless the Lord ordains it," goes that line of thinking, which I tend to favor when we're talking about *my* death. But before those rational, truth-filled thoughts prevail, I'm temporarily held captive by the lies that my days are short and I'll never see eighty years of age. I must replace those thoughts with a simple truth. *I'm not destined to die*, I think instead—and sometimes I even say it aloud to myself—*I'm destined to live.*

I'm not destined to die; I'm destined to live. In my weakness, Christ makes me strong—these ideas catch my breath.

The fact is, I've already outlived the prognosis every doctor in my life has given me. Given my congenital heart condition, I should really be dead already.

Just last week a physician friend of mine was introducing me to a new ministry board member. He said to the man, "This is Brady Boyd, and we're pretty much just happy to have him with us." Then he looked at me and said, "We're so happy to have you with us, Brady. Really. You're one of the first people to make it to forty-nine years old with the exact condition you have."

I looked at him with an expression that said, "Um, *thanks?*"

Then he looked back at our new board member and said, "This guy's a cool study for us docs."

The delivery may have been a little crass, but the content was 100 percent true. When I was a child, heart doctors told my parents I'd never see my teenage years. *Tetralogy of Fallot* they call it, which equates to a cardiac anomaly reflecting not one or two or three heart defects but *four.* It's something you don't want to have. And yet thanks to modern medicine and some highly competent docs, here I sit today, writing a book at age forty-nine.

But that fleeting, flagellating self-talk is really tempting to believe. *Your heart is weak. You're going to have a heart attack. You're going to die young.* Praise God for decatastrophization. Our self-talk can be made new. *God, you be strong in me where I fear I'm weak,* I tell him. *You've numbered my days, Father. Help me make them count.*

THE CURE FOR THE INSECURE

As I mentioned, part of the reason it's critical to get a handle on our self-talk is that it determines whether we'll stand firm or fall apart in the face of Satan's taunts. The stakes are too high for us to waste time believing lies. When we spend our energies nursing our inadequacies or begging for the spotlight or trying to keep a leg up on the competition—whoever or whatever that might be—we forfeit every noble opportunity to live life as God meant us to live it.

Think about it: it's tough to engage in healthy relationships when you're always sizing people up, touting the ways you're better than they are, and putting them in their place whenever they threaten your authority or expertise. The Bible says we're to consider others' needs before we consider our own (see Phil. 2:3–4) and that we are to prioritize loving others and serving others and being hospitable to others and forgiving others when they screw up—all of which prove really challenging when we're committed to self-condemnation.

It has been said that we treat others in the same manner we treat ourselves; if that's true—and I believe it is—then our feelings of self-reproach will eventually cause us to reproach others as well. Just *try* connecting in life-giving community with the same people you've chosen to condemn. It makes the small-group experience awkward, at best, for you can't love those you've decided to hate.

This brings me to a realization I've come to over the course of the past year or so. Given my firsthand experience with insecurity, I've had a lot of time to reflect on its signs (how it shows up) and its solution (how it gets extracted once and for all). While I'm 100 percent confident in the treatment plan I'm about to offer you, I can almost guarantee you won't like my cure. If you wrestle with insecurity—and truly, at one time or another I believe all of us do—then

I urge you to read the next paragraph carefully. Your ability to relate well with God, your confidence in standing up to the lies of the Enemy, and your capacity for initiating, maintaining, and adding value to key relationships hinge on this one crucial step.

If negative self-talk is taking you down on a frequent basis— that is, if you're constantly stacking up your life to others' lives and determining that you just don't measure up, or else you're known to pounce on any open pause in a conversation to trump what the other person just said, or you're convinced that everyone in the world is out to get you, and you take it upon yourself to get them first—then one of two things is to blame (I'm going to use strong language here, but please stick around to hear me out):

- You're showing a tendency toward being an immature fool who refuses to be taught.
- You're simply childlike in your faith and in need of spiritual and emotional help.

If negative agreements are eating you for lunch every day, then you need to either wise up or grow up—sometimes maybe even both. Shame is often to blame here; we've got to banish the shame.

THE COST OF SHAME

Underneath insecurity, regardless of whether we're talking about spiritual insecurity (caused by our own lack of life experience or perhaps because we suffered abuse in our past), can lurk a pervasive sense of shame. It can come from feeling we don't know enough, we haven't done enough, we aren't valuable enough—basically that in some way, shape, or form, *we are just not enough*. And our list of shortcomings can go on and on.

And to clarify, I am not saying that shame is necessarily some-thing you brought on yourself—you may have suffered terrible abuse in earlier years, whether it was sexual, psychological, verbal, physical, or other types of mistreatment. In both cases—shame thrust upon us through trauma or brought out through our own insecurities—God is there, and he wants us to be healed and whole.

Last spring, after reading Dr. Brené Brown's thought-provoking book *Daring Greatly*, I devoted a weekly staff meeting to the subject of shame. Dr. Brown has spent the sum of her career studying the weighty topics of shame and vulnerability. According to Brown and other mental-health professionals, shame is the "master emotion." It's rooted in the fear that we aren't good enough, and its implications are severe. Shame erodes courage, spurs self-hatred, inspires a proliferation of unhelpful comparisons with others, and fuels disengagement. Dr. Brown delivered a TED Talk in Houston in 2010 titled "The Power of Vulnerability," which, at this writing, has been viewed more than twenty million times. I loved her book. I loved her TED Talk. I loved her invitation to practice more responsible vulnerability patterns. And I loved the idea of exposing my staff to the themes therein. And so, the meeting.

Over a period of several months, it came to my attention that our staff was sitting on good ideas. We would have meetings and lunchtime conversations, hallway chats and performance reviews, and yet regardless of the myriad discussion forums in play, we weren't getting the best thinking from even our longest-tenured folks. I did some digging, and what I discovered troubled me. As it turned out, our staff was playing it safe for fear of rejection, retribution, and being mocked. (My colleagues and I work at a *church*, I should remind you. They thought they'd be rejected or ridiculed *here*, in this *safe, loving environment*?) Something had to be done.

I opened the staff meeting with Dr. Brown's twenty-minute TED Talk, and then I summarized her findings for our staff. I then divided our team into fifteen groups of ten and said, "We're going to have a little competition, and each group is going to have a winner. Furthermore, each winner is going to be handed a crisp one-hundred-dollar bill."

There had been some fidgeting in the room while the video played—people checking their cell phones, women digging through their purses, various folks slipping out for a restroom break—but at the mention of cold, hard cash, all eyes were on me. "Today I'm going to pay you for a good idea," I continued. "Within your table group, I want each of you to complete this sentence: 'New Life Church would be even better if …' Once your group hears each member's idea, you need to reach a consensus on which idea is the best, and that's the idea you'll present to the team at large. You have thirty minutes to think, deliberate, and prepare your presentation. Ready? Go."

And with that the teams were off.

I migrated around the room as teams jotted down innovative thoughts, began fighting for their best ideas, and wrestled good-naturedly over which to present. As I meandered from table to table, I heard a fair amount of hedging: "You guys may think this is stupid, but …" or "I don't really have any standout ideas, but here's something I thought of …" or "This seems kind of silly, but …"

Sharing new ideas always requires vulnerability; everyone feels foolish at first. But nothing good comes from stuffing our thoughts and playing small. Every world-changing innovation—the radio, the lightbulb, air travel, you name it—was considered foolish at first or was developed from a concept that was initially flawed and didn't work. I encouraged my team with as much enthusiasm and compassion as I could. "It takes a lot of courage to do what you guys are doing," I said as I roamed. "Thank you for engaging in this."

The other incentive I'd mentioned in my opening remarks was that a grand-prize winner would be selected from the pool of group winners, and that person would receive five hundred dollars. Given what was on the line, people were quickly sidestepping their insecurity, shame, and awkwardness and going to bat for their solutions and ideas.

In the end, despite the fact it cost me a cool two grand, that staff meeting netted nearly immeasurable benefits. On the financial side, our leadership team regained the two-thousand-dollar investment that very week, and the grand-prize-winning idea *alone* realized more than one hundred thousand dollars in savings over the next six months. Emotionally the tenor in the room was the brightest and most energetic I'd seen it in months. And spiritually I knew that God was breaking down barriers that had siloed our ministry groups away from each other for years. But the biggest gain wasn't financial, emotional, or spiritual in nature; it was *conversational*. In the span of that one-hour meeting, our staff's messaging functions were overhauled, beginning with the messages we'd been speaking over ourselves.

Over the ensuing days and weeks, more and more staffers approached me to tell me what a life-changing experience that meeting had been. To substantiate their assessments, they highlighted the genius insights from Dr. Brown, the levity that the payout created, and the sheer joy of brainstorming with their peers. But what struck me most about their follow-up comments were their acknowledgments that shame-filled self-talk had fueled the dysfunction in the first place.

Because they thought, *I'll be seen as a tattletale*, they let expensive inefficiencies mount. Because they thought, *I'll be seen as judgmental*, they let real congregational needs go unaddressed. Because they thought, *I'll be seen as the jerk who always throws stones*, they let archaic approaches to ministry corrode our church. And so, instead of showing up with their best evaluations, their best opinions, their best contributions—their best *selves*—they'd been stuffing all the good ideas and letting fear and mediocrity win the day.

In the same way Adam and Eve hid from God as a result of the shame they felt, our staff had been hiding out, waiting for the shame storm to pass. The shameful messages they'd bought into proved costly in every way, and escaping those messages helped our entire congregation as well as many in our community.

BREAKING THE LOOP OF LOSS

Any of us who were glued to our television screens the week of September 11, 2001, remembers the incessant loop of video footage of the planes hitting the two World Trade Center towers and the horrifying images and effects as those towers fell. We can call it up from memory even now and describe in vivid detail the bluebird sky, the shocking impact, the concrete raining down from the heavens as New York City ran for its collective life. We know the scenes by heart because they were seared into our consciousness that week. It's a dynamic Satan loves to employ—let's call it the "loop of loss"—and it feeds our tendency toward negative self-talk:

- *If I tell them my idea, they'll think I'm stupid.*
- *If I take a risk, I'll surely fail.*
- *If they really knew me, they wouldn't love me.*
- *Given the truth about me, I'm better off playing small.*

The content of the messages isn't as important as the tone, which is disparaging, and the frequency, which is constant. Relentless reproach is the name of the Enemy's game. When we count ourselves out as losers, he wins.

The table-group idea that took the five-hundred-dollar prize at that staff meeting last spring—the one that netted our church more than one hundred thousand dollars in short-term cost savings—centered on sharing resources across our entire ministry instead of stockpiling department-specific resources. We have a giant basement at New Life that is used largely for storage, and over time each department had laid claim to a separate little corner of that basement and cordoned off "their stuff," which was, by definition, nobody else's stuff.

Supply needs would arise for one event or another, but because the group in need of those supplies didn't know that we as a church already owned what they needed, they would go buy duplicate supplies. One situation comes to mind in which a ministry team spent several hundred dollars to buy coolers for an overnight father-son camping trip they were coordinating, because they had no idea that our student ministry possessed seven coolers already that weren't being used during the camping dates.

It felt very "Acts 2" of us on the day we cleaned out the massive basement, centralized our resources, and created a system whereby any department in need could simply "go shopping" for what they needed in our own pile of stuff. No more hoarding, no more "mine" mentality, no more money tossed to the wind. It was a really, really good day.

That day got me thinking about the costs involved in living from a place of shame—not just the monetary ones but the incalculable ones as well. What expense am I bearing—in my relationships, in my career, in my soul—when I buy into the message that I'm not enough, or that I'm destined for failure, or that forgiveness is out of reach?

I suspect that if we could quantify that expense, it would bankrupt the richest of men.

After the shooting at New Life, I went through a period of several months when I couldn't consume any media violence whatsoever. Before the event, I had enjoyed watching the TV series *24*, for instance, but with all of the sights and sounds of that horrific day pounding through my mind and heart, I had to take a break. The same was true of action movies—I couldn't bear the sound of gunfire, and I couldn't stomach the sight of blood. My sensitivities were so heightened during that season that I needed to be extra vigilant about the input I allowed. Reinforcement of the ideas that life was scary, humanity was brutal, and evil was lurking behind every tree was the very last thing I needed back then.

I have friends who have all but sworn off R-rated movies for largely the same reason. Somewhere along the way they realized that if they subject themselves to certain language and images, it's harder for them to think pure thoughts and abide by the standard of uprightness they value. The plot may be fantastic, but if the presentation is marked by crassness, cruelty, or darkness, they're out. Those characteristics start forming agreements in them that are never helpful in the end.

I know of people who spend a significant chunk of their paychecks each month on professional therapy. Someone said something cruel to them when they were children that they're now trying to undo as adults. Still others have inched away from certain friendships after realizing that those particular friends were the opposite of life giving. Instead, they tended to be dramatic, cynical, discouraging, or down.

I've served at New Life for eight years now, and I continue to excavate reasons our staff has been struggling with shame, reasons that in some cases are decades old. I keep picking at the issues because I know it's a worthwhile dig. Shame and the negative agreements that emerge from it will continue to overtake the thought-life garden unless they are pulled up by the roots. Once those tangled roots surface and are tossed into the trash, however, we'll know a freedom we've never felt before. Over time the seeds of positive agreements we plant will produce strong shoots of sureness that will enable us to resemble Jesus Christ.

TUNING IN | CHAPTER 5
Respond

1. Can you relate to the idea of not measuring up in some aspect of your life? How do such feelings hamstring your ability to stand up to the Enemy's taunts?

2. When are you most tempted to self-promote? Why does self-promotion feel more satisfying than waiting on God to "lift you up in due time," as 1 Peter 5:6 says?

3. What situations (hypothetical or real), people, or assumptions about the world threaten your sense of "all-right-ness"?

Reflect

Spend several minutes thinking about what your negative self-talk has cost you along the way. Time? Energy? Opportunities for advancement? Relationships that were important to you? Inner peace? Something else?

Read On

Read the full account of Jesus and Pilate found in John 19. How powerful do you suppose God truly is? Do you believe that his power is available to you today?

6

TAKING GOD AT HIS WORD

Believe the story and you'll finally enter it for yourself.
—Steven James, *Story: Recapture the Mystery*

I often talk with people about this pattern of shifting from negative, destructive self-talk to that which is positive and fueled by truth. I explain my belief that as we practice meditating on God's Word, whenever weak thoughts get into our minds, we can ask God to exchange them for strong ones. We don't have to allow lies to beat us up and beat us down any longer; we can walk in freedom—we really can.

On occasion the people I'm talking with light up and say, "Makes perfect sense. I'll give it a try." And then they do give it a try. Sometime later they report back to me that the tide of their self-talk has turned and caused them to experience greater optimism and joy.

I celebrate those stories! They represent my own story of moving from lies to truth in terms of how I tend to speak to myself. But those stories don't reflect the most common responses I hear.

The typical reaction to my little self-talk diatribe is this: "Eh. It's just a phase. I'm sure it will pass."

What these folks don't realize, of course, is that our negative self-talk *doesn't* pass. No, it only increases in force until we wake up one day not motivated enough to get out of bed and wondering what on earth happened to us. How did we get *here*?

Think of it this way: negative thoughts are like open apps on your phone; they drain your battery until you close them. Each time you and I choose to come to God with our weak self-talk ("I'm a loser." "I'm a failure." "Nobody cares.") and ask him to replace it with truth ("I'm chosen." "I'm beloved." "God sees me." "God cares."), we're in effect shutting down the thing that's draining our inner-strength batteries dry. Keep swiping those energy-sucking agreements shut, and even at the end of the longest day, you'll have some oomph to spare.

The point here is that the war on harmful self-talk doesn't get won unless we show up ready for the fight. Negative self-talk won't quiet itself; it simply has to be overcome. And the battle strategy I've seen work best by far is to hit it with a few rounds of God's Word.

I KNOW HE CAN

I was watching TV the other night when a Hormel commercial came on. The product being pushed was their new Rev deli-meat wrap, and the script centered on the looped phrase *I think I can, I think I can*. We see a basketball player dribbling a ball, a skateboarder preparing for a jump, and a football player running drills. Over the footage we hear with escalating speed and volume, "I … think … I can … I THINK I can … I THINK I CAN!" The athletes rip open a

Rev-Pack just before executing whatever sports move they're about to make, and then, ostensibly as a result of the sixteen grams of protein they've just ingested, they experience wild and immediate success.

It got me thinking: Is biblical self-talk any different from chanting "I think I can … I think I can" on the playing field called life?

Take a look around you—in bookstores and online, on the radio and on the lips of well-meaning friends—and you'll see and hear similar sentiments everywhere. "If you can dream it, you can do it," one author purports. "We were all called to do great things for God!" a motivational speaker cheers.

"Live your best life now!"

"Success is waiting for you!"

"You can—and *you will*!"

There in front of my TV, I thought back to the days following the shooting at our church campus in 2007. One hundred days into my tenure as senior pastor, a gunman unknown to our church community showed up as morning worship services were concluding and inexplicably opened fire, randomly killing two teenagers and injuring several other members. It was senseless, it was tragic, and it ushered in a season of intense grief and exhaustion for us all.

As the leader of our congregation, I found the burden of communication resting on my shoulders, and I can assure you that what carried me through that period was not a fluffy "I think I can" sentiment. No, what steadied my stance and bolstered my faith were the words of Psalm 23:4: "Even though I walk through the darkest valley, I will fear no evil, for you are with me; your rod and your staff, they comfort me."

This situation is dark, but I don't have to be afraid.

I'm not alone.

God sees me.

God is with me.

God will provide comfort at every turn.

"I think I can" doesn't empower a person. When the burden for winning the battles of life is on our shoulders, we will fail. But transfer that weight to the mighty shoulders of God, and it's a whole new discussion. *God* is the One who created us. *God* is the One who sustains us. *God* is the one who delivers us. *God* gives us a future and a hope. Trust *him* to teach you how to feel toward yourself, and you'll start crushing negative agreements left and right.

SETTING CHRIST APART AS LORD

After I surrendered my life to Christ as a teenager, I made a habit of reading my Bible almost every day. I would choose a passage of Scripture and sit quietly with it until I'd made my way through those verses, one by one, slowly and methodically, trying as hard as I could to absorb what the words were saying. Then I would do nothing for a few minutes, just letting the ideas wash over me. The primary benefit of growing up in the care of a father (and a mother) who lavished words of encouragement and confidence on me— *"Brady, I love you and I'm proud of you. You're smart, Son, and you can do anything in life you want to do."*—was that it taught me how to accept words of praise from God.

When I came to a Scripture passage about the love of God or the protection of God or the provision God makes in believers' lives, I had no problem seeing myself as the recipient of those good things. I'd read of God calling his children his sheep or his beloved ones or his friends, and I'd think, *I'm all those things to God? How cool.* These days

I commit myself to affirming my kids so that they will someday enjoy this same dynamic of reading Scripture and actually believing that all those promises aren't for some nameless, faceless somebody out there; those promises are for *them*.

In the pages of God's Word, I learned that he has plans for me that are hopeful and good (see Jer. 29:11); that when life feels unbearable, he will carry my burdens for me and let me rest (see Matt. 11:28–29); that no matter how substantial my list of needs is, Jesus can meet them all (see Phil. 4:19); and that as long as I listen to God, I can live every day in peace (see Prov. 1:33).

As I sat with these ideas and let them seep into my head and heart, something uncanny began to happen: despite my less-than-great life experiences, the meanness of other people from time to time, and the deep suspicions I had that I didn't quite measure up, the power of all this truth began to overtake my thoughts. I could utterly change my self-talk by letting God's Word inch its way in.

While talking about how to cultivate inner-world steadiness and sturdiness, the apostle Peter used an interesting phrase. In 1 Peter 3:15, he says we should "set Christ apart ... as Lord." The full sentence says, "In your hearts set Christ apart [as holy—acknowledging Him, giving Him first place in your lives] as Lord" (AMP).

Now this exhortation comes on the heels of Peter's overarching plea for living a righteous life. Quoting the book of Psalms, he said,

> The one who wants to enjoy life and see good days
> [good—whether apparent or not],
> Must keep his tongue free from evil and his lips
> from speaking guile (treachery, deceit).

He must turn away from wickedness and do what
is right.
He must search for peace [with God, with self,
with others] and pursue it eagerly [actively—not
merely desiring it].

For the eyes of the Lord are [looking favorably]
upon the righteous (the upright),
And His ears are attentive to their prayer (eager
to answer),
But the face of the Lord is against those who
practice evil. (vv. 10–12 AMP)

I emphasized the amplification about searching for peace
because it's relevant to our discussion. If we want to extricate harmful self-talk from our lives altogether, we have to make peace not just
with God and with others but also *with ourselves*. And the way we
get that done is by choosing to set Christ apart as Lord.

To set Christ apart as Lord is to declare him master over our
lives, which are comprised of our actions, which are steered by our
words, which are born in our thoughts. When he is set apart as Lord
over our thoughts, other things can't be in charge. When Christ
is Lord over our thoughts, depression can't also be lord. Fear can't
also be lord. Anxiety can't also be lord. Diminishment can't also be
lord. Self-reproach can't also be lord. *Nothing* else can be lord of our
thoughts *when we have set Christ apart as Lord of our everything*.

And we're to do this not once but over and over again. Starting
my day with my morning prayer helps me get off on the right foot

in this regard. Take today, for instance. I woke at six and noticed it was raining, which is not an overly common occurrence in the high desert of Colorado. I made a cup of coffee, headed for the back deck, and plopped down on one of the deck chairs, eager to watch the storm unfold.

As I took in the sheets of moisture peppering the dry ground below while I stayed dry beneath our awning, I said my morning prayer, including the part about setting Christ apart as Lord. What a refreshing way to start the day and, in this case, the workweek. Setting Christ apart as Lord in my heart had the same effect as rain on parched earth.

When I'm really thinking through this idea that Christ is set apart as Lord, my meetings go much better. My self-talk sounds much better. Everything goes much better.

Later this morning I had to work alongside another leader at New Life and make some difficult staffing decisions. It was a tough discussion, but it unfolded easily—due in large part, I feel sure, to the fact that I had intentionally set Christ apart as Lord hours before it occurred.

And so, in the same way I remind my kids (every single day, day after day after day) to pick up their clothes, brush their teeth, walk the dog, do their homework, and *Please!* put on deodorant so those practices will be ingrained into the rhythm of their days, I come before God each morning and tell him, *I set you apart as Lord.* To build helpful self-talk patterns, I have to set apart the right One for the right reasons for a very, very long time.

Persistence pays. The day will come when you wake up with the realization that, just as your computer's spell-checker instantaneously types *right* when you've errantly written *rihgt*, when Jesus is set apart as Lord of your thoughts, he lovingly guides the firing of your mental synapses, setting every formation "right" in the same way.

THE QUESTION THAT SUBDUES OUR SELF-TALK

Throughout my day I ask myself a question as often as possible in the hope of keeping negative agreements at bay. This question has kept me out of the ditch on more occasions than I can count and is the safety net that runs underneath my life at all times, guaranteeing it will catch me in the event I fall. The question is this: *How does this thought I'm thinking, this assumption I'm building, or this agreement I'm making line up with the Word of God?*

If the thought, assumption, or agreement squares with truth, it can stay; if not, it has to go—it doesn't get any simpler than that.

Throughout the Bible—all the way from Genesis to Revelation—warfare imagery is evoked, and in ten out of ten of those occurrences, God is referring not merely to battles fought with hands and feet and horses and shields and swords but to battles fought in our *minds*. This idea is what was at the core of the apostle Paul's exhortation to the Corinthian church to "demolish arguments and every pretension that sets itself up against the knowledge of God" (2 Cor. 10:5). The "demolishment," according to Paul, would occur as those Christ followers took "captive every thought to make it obedient to Christ," language considered strong (violent, even?) to first-century ears.

In Paul's day, one of the ways Roman forces intimidated conquered cities was to chain the governors and other leaders of those cities and parade them through the streets, indisputably conveying the message, "Your situation is helpless and hopeless! Even your leaders have been defeated and shamed. Rome is here to stay." Roman conquerors were masters of the siege, going to any lengths—starvation, humiliation, rape, and death—to take over the world. It is this imagery Paul looked to when describing how we are to conquer our thoughts.

"Take them captive!" Paul insisted. "Strip them naked until they are totally exposed. Bring them to a place of earnest submission, no holds barred."

The stakes were high for cities that Rome was overtaking, and the stakes are high for us too. If we don't overtake our own negative agreements, proving their impotence by parading them through the streets, they will fight with all they have to exert their will on us. Thoughts become words, words become actions, actions become habits, and habits form who we are. To take our thoughts captive is to consciously declare whether our lives will be governed by truth or by lies.

SO, WHAT DOES THE WORD OF GOD SAY?

Of course, eradicating harmful self-talk by taking our thoughts captive so we can evaluate how they stack up "against the knowledge of God"—as 2 Corinthians 10:5 says to do—is predicated on our first *knowing* the knowledge of God. We can't gauge a thought's worthiness in light of God's Word if we don't have a clue what it says, which is why it's so valuable to devote time to reading the Bible. The minutes you invest in absorbing what's true about God—and about you—are minutes you're not falling for lies. Plus, there's an X factor to time spent with God. He says that the time you give him will never return void.

Are you ready for a cool promise? Read the following verses about God slowly and meditatively, even if this is the umpteenth time you've seen them:

> As the rain and the snow
>> come down from heaven,
> and do not return to it
>> without watering the earth
> and making it bud and flourish,
>> so that it yields seed for the sower and bread
>>> for the eater,
> so is my word that goes out from my mouth:
>> It will not return to me empty,
> but will accomplish what I desire
>> and achieve the purpose for which I sent it.
> You will go out in joy
>> and be led forth in peace;
> the mountains and hills
>> will burst into song before you,
> and all the trees of the field
>> will clap their hands.
> Instead of the thornbush will grow the juniper,
>> and instead of briers the myrtle will grow.

> This will be for the LORD's renown,
>> for an everlasting sign,
>> that will endure forever. (Isa. 55:10–13)

Listen, when God speaks, those words *count*. He assures us they don't come back empty. Instead, they accomplish the purpose for which he sent them. Do you know what God's purpose is? *Restoration*—of *all* things—which, by definition, includes you and me. He sent Jesus to create a way to relate directly with us because he loves us and is committed to spending eternity with us.

And so when he speaks to us—which is exactly what happens whenever we open his Word and meditate on what is written there—it's for the purpose of drawing us near, of renewing our minds, of winning our hearts, of confirming truth, of reminding us who we are and whose we are and why we're on this great big ball called Earth. His words send us out in joy, lead us out in peace, and change us from the inside out.

So: *read. Read* God's Word. Get into it so that it can get into you. Commit yourself to the practice of learning your Father's heart. It will transform your self-talk. As Christ followers, we read Scripture not to check off an obligatory to-do for the day or fulfill a ritual each morning but instead *to learn how to speak to ourselves only the words God would have us speak.*

If my self-talk tells me I'm not seen or valued, but God's Word says I am (see Ps. 139:13–16, for instance), then the truth is *I am.*

If my self-talk tells me I don't have a future or a hope, but God's Word says I do (see Jer. 29:11), then the truth is *I do.*

If my self-talk tells me I won't make it through whatever storm is threatening to take me under, but God's Word says I will (see 2 Cor. 12:9), then the truth is *I will*.

Reading the Bible isn't just a good habit. When we read the Bible, we read truth and memorize truth and absorb truth day by day *so that our self-talk will be true*.

Because I was familiar with the words of Psalm 23, in the hours immediately following the shooting at New Life, I was able to summon those Scriptures and chew on them instead of chewing on my nails. The honest truth? I was freaked out beyond belief. Our local universe seemed to be spinning out of control, and I felt wholly unequipped to handle what was being thrown my way in terms of communications needs, logistical decisions, and knowing how to help people react emotionally and spiritually.

And yet in a matter of moments, there was that verse—*poof!*—right in the center of my thoughts. *I will fear no evil*, I said to nobody but myself there in my office as bad news kept lighting up my phone. *I will fear no evil. I will fear no evil. I will fear no evil.* Nothing else could get through to my consciousness, because I'd jammed up my mental airwaves with truth.

Several days later, when our congregation gathered to mourn the loss of two of our own and to call out to God as a body broken, I stood on the platform and said, "We will not be governed by fear." I meant it. Yes, the unthinkable had happened in our midst. Yes, it was tragic and unnerving and terrifying as it unfolded. Yes, laying two wonderful teenagers to rest long before their lives should have ended was agonizing for us all. But God was still God, his presence was still real, and victory was still his in the end. "Even though we are walking through a dark valley," I assured those gathered, "we will fear no evil, for you, God, are with us! Your rod and your staff, they comfort us."

Do you see the progression here? I wouldn't have been able to encourage our congregation had I not first heard from heaven and allowed God to reset my self-talk according to the truth. The same is true for you: you will never relate well with others if you haven't first related well with God, the inspirer of every wise syllable we think or speak.

As you consider beginning the practice of reading God's Word regularly and then taking God at his word in your everyday life—about who you are, about why you're here, about the value you bring to life, and about the things he'd love to hear you say, both to him and to the people around you—I'd like to give you a few self-talk statements to ponder, truths taken right from the Word of God. If you're struggling today to overcome a negative agreement you've made, try repeating one of the following three insights slowly in your spirit. Speak truth over yourself and your situation, and see what God might do.

"I'm made on purpose, for a purpose."

Truth number one is this: you were made on purpose, for a purpose. You were no accident, and your life today is not in vain.

Now, if you wrestle with believing this one, you're not alone. Even men and women who spent time with Jesus when he was a living, breathing human being ministering here on planet Earth struggled to understand their purpose in life. After his resurrection, during a forty-day period when Jesus continued to teach his followers about all that was to come as eternity began to unfold, he reminded them that he hadn't come to free them from Roman oppression; his mission wasn't a geopolitical one. Instead, he told them he had come to establish the kingdom of God, and that he had chosen *them* to cooperate with him in its unveiling. Even with Jesus there—alive from the dead—telling them right to their faces, they still couldn't understand.

As Jesus reached the end of his time on the earth and was preparing to ascend to heaven, his followers asked him if maybe *now* was when he was going to restore the kingdom to Israel. *Again* they were trolling for a political leg up, when Jesus's only claims had been spiritual in nature. Jesus looked at his beloved followers and said, "Guys, listen. Let's go over this one more time. You will receive power when the Holy Spirit comes on you, and you will be my witnesses in Jerusalem and in all of Judea and in Samaria and to the ends of the earth, but I *did not* show up to set up the kingdom of Israel. I came to set up the kingdom of heaven on earth. And I'm hoping you'll join that cause."

Jesus looked his men in the eye and said, "If you're in, then *go*. Go to Jerusalem. Go to Judea. Go to Samaria. Take this message of grace all over the world."

And then he ascended into the clouds, an act that had to totally floor the people still tethered to the earth. Not only had they never seen someone get lifted into another realm, but emotionally they had to be jarred. "Wait! Where are you going?" they probably hollered. "The Romans! The Romans are still here!"

The Bible says that while this supposed hollering was going on, two angels appeared to confirm to the incredulous onlookers exactly what Jesus had said to do. "Why are you staring into the sky, when you have an assignment?" they asked. "Go back to Jerusalem and wait" (see Acts 1:3–11).

Quit standing around. Wait on the Holy Spirit. And then tell the world about me! This was the first-century follower's life purpose, and it remains our purpose today, even if we rarely see things that way. Most of us are just a *tiny* bit self-centered, self-focused, and self-consumed, so the idea that our entire existence is to hinge on something or someone other than ourselves is disconcerting, to say the least. And yet it's here, in the center of saying yes to cooperating with Jesus's mission, that we find the fulfillment we're looking for.

Ultimately, the kingdom of God will be completely established, and you and I will be able to enjoy all the benefits of heaven for all eternity—but that's not the plan right now. The plan right now is for us to be mobilized, empowered, and sent.

As you work to turn around your self-talk, try praying along these lines:

> *Father, I don't know what you want to do in my family or my neighborhood or my workplace or my city today, but I'm here to cooperate with your plan. Please show me where your kingdom is coming to earth today, and tell me how I can be a part of what you are doing.*

I get asked about big-ticket issues frequently: "When do you think the economy will turn around?" "How will terrorist groups finally be defeated?" "Why is there such an attack on the institution of marriage these days?" and so forth. My answer rarely sits well with the person who inquired. "Do you want to know when the economy will turn around?" I say. "It will turn around when God finds enough people in this country who are willing to cooperate with him."

I mean every syllable of that response. The economy will turn around when God finds enough people who will cooperate with his activity instead of spending their income (and then some) on themselves. Terrorism will be put in its place when God finds enough people who will cooperate with his activity instead of insulating and isolating themselves in fear. Marriage will be favored in society when God finds enough people who will cooperate with his activity instead of pursuing pleasure apart from their spouses.

Outright miracles will unfold in our midst when enough of us come back to our God-ordained purpose in life. We're not cosmic accidents; we're divinely crafted for a world-changing purpose, which is to put words and actions to the love of Christ. This is where fulfillment is found.

"I'm loved."

A second truth to reinforce in your mind and heart is that you are loved. *You. Are. Loved.* Let those words sink in. You don't have to beg for love, conjure up love, perform for love, or pay for whatever facsimile of love you're considering. Deep, abiding, unconditional, unchanging, free-of-charge love is yours for the taking. *Almighty God loves you.*

At least once a month, someone from our congregation—usually a man—seeks me out to confess an addiction to porn. If I tried to count the number of men I've met over the years who struggle with viewing inappropriate websites, I'd glaze over in minutes, I'm sure. I myself have battled pornography along the way and have been open about it in my teaching, which is perhaps why so many men ask to meet with me.

Pornography is a horrible affliction for a man to deal with, especially in the Christian world. If a good, godly man is caught looking at porn, he's doomed—in his mind, at least. Viewing degrading images of women (or worse still, children) represents, to many Christian men, giving in to the lowest levels of human depravity, and to be caught in such an addiction is extremely embarrassing and even debilitating.

So instead of reaching out for the help he obviously needs, a man will stuff his feelings, deny his problem, and try to move on with his life, thinking he can overcome his addiction by sheer willpower. Why? Because he has played out the confession scenario in his mind and determined that the fallout from "coming out of the basement" will be too great.

He believes that if anyone finds out what he's been doing, they'll disrespect him, disregard him, and treat him like the degenerate he feels he is. He fears that his wife and kids will leave him, his boss will fire him, and everyone who knows him will see him as nothing more than pond scum for the rest of his life.

For this reason, when a man *does* seek me out and *does* confess his addiction to porn, I always say the same thing: "This bondage is going to be broken because you have taken a really courageous first step. You will live free from this addiction. You will not have to struggle with this awfulness. In Christ, you have a new identity.

This isn't who you really are. You are loved by God—do you realize that? I want you to remind yourself of these truths this week. You need to repeat over and over to yourself these phrases: 'I am loved.' 'I am chosen.' 'I am satisfied in Christ.'"

Many of those men return weeks or months later to update me on how things are going, and before they say a word, I can see their progress reflected in their eyes. I can tell who has been believing the truth about God's love for them and who has not. When we believe deep down that we are radically, irrationally, unconditionally, exuberantly loved by the One who really counts, it changes everything we think, everything we say, and everything we do.

When we believe we're loved, we quit searching for love in other places—or what *feels* like love, anyway. Sinful tendencies and addictions start to get subdued because the void has been beautifully filled. When we turn to God instead of turning to the offerings of the world, he won't rebuke us (see Zeph. 3:17), and we are quieted by his love, the Scriptures say, like a baby who's just been fed (see Ps. 131:2).

"In Christ, I will prevail."

I caught a documentary recently featuring tornado survivors from Moore, Oklahoma, a town that sustained a deadly F5 twister with wind speeds reaching more than two hundred miles per hour. Official sources reported that twenty-four people were killed the day that storm barreled through town, but that only reflects *physical* death. Emotionally, countless others were slain. The story I found most haunting was of a young boy who had been so traumatized over the loss of his sister, who died when their house collapsed in on them, that still today, years after the event, he cowers in fear whenever he hears even a distant clap of thunder or catches sight of lightning zigzagging its way across the sky. His family says he absolutely won't come outside if it's raining, and he visibly shakes until the sun shines again.

No matter who you are or what you've been through, you either believe that *in Christ* you are powerful enough to overcome every shadow of darkness you encounter, or you believe you are subject to every whim of that darkness. The darkness could look like fear, as was the case with the boy in Oklahoma, or it could be something else entirely. Compulsion, addiction, anxiety and depression, self-defeat, narcissism, anger, pride—anything that sets itself up as a stumbling block along the path of righteousness qualifies. The question is, *can we overcome?*

There are days when I succumb to things that rob me of my livelihood and strength, and I'm left feeling exhausted, wrung out, and weak. On those days I have to remember that because of the One who lives inside me, I am more powerful than I know. The Bible says that those who love God are equipped with "the sword of the Spirit, which is the word of God" (Eph. 6:17). In other words, on days when we're lacking power, we can go to God's Word and gain strength.

A friend gifted me with a giant *Braveheart*-looking sword one time, which I keep in a corner of my office. My colleagues at the church know that if they happen by my window and see a big blade swooshing through the air, Pastor Brady must be having a rough day.

We all need to be reminded from time to time that as we read Scripture and meditate on Scripture and let the truths of Scripture seep into our lives, we become a force to be reckoned with in the spiritual realm, where the real battles of life are fought. We advance God's kingdom in direct proportion to our faithfulness to read, pray, and speak his Word.

First John 4:4 says, "You, dear children, are from God and have overcome them [*John is referring here to evil spirits that vie for our attention*], because the one who is in you is greater than the one who is in the world." We are powerful because Jesus is powerful. Of course, you and I can still rattle off all our weaknesses—those foibles, flaws, and idiosyncrasies we wish we could banish from our lives—but instead of operating from that place of weakness, we should say, *God, please be my power*, and then move forward in that newfound strength.

STEADFASTNESS AND JOY

Not long ago I took some time off and traveled a few states over to the bank of a river I knew as a boy. There beside the grandeur of that flowing water, it seemed as if God wanted to say something to me. It took me a few minutes to still my body and quiet my heart—the RPMs never slow very easily—but eventually I felt myself open up to his voice.

In my spirit I heard him say, *Brady, you're very committed to your assignment, and that's a good thing. You're passionate about your work, and that's a good thing. You deeply love the people you're pastoring, and that's a good thing. But, Brady? You've lost your joy.*

Not surprisingly, it was the truth. A lot of bad news had unfolded in our community and in the world at large over the previous month, and the effect on me had been profound. I'd been faithful to my calling, to my family, and to my church, even as I was pretty much down in the dumps. At the river's edge, I thought about the words of Psalm 51, where David asked God, "Create in me a clean heart … and renew a steadfast spirit within me." He then added, "Restore to me the joy of Your salvation" (vv. 10, 12 NASB). That's what I needed: *pure joy.*

Whatever our assignments and roles are—spouse, leader, parent, employee, student, sibling, mentor, friend—we can be people who reflect not only diligence in our work but also the *joy of Christ* in our hearts. We can bypass negative agreements in favor of buying into truth. We can refuse to lower our heads when times get tough, choosing instead to listen up, look up, and lift our heads to God. We can write God's Word on the tablets of our hearts and walk in the power that is promised therein for those who are committed to Christ.

When I landed back in Colorado after those days at the river, the mountains looked more beautiful than they'd ever looked before. The air felt crisper. The trees seemed greener. None of these things had *actually* changed from when I had been there days earlier, of course; it's just that I had new lenses through which to see. In the Desperation Band song "Take Me to the River," there's a line that says, "As I wait within the swell / You sweep away what's of myself."[1] It's a good articulation of how God's truth purifies our inner beliefs.

It's purification we desperately need if we're ever to stand firm against Satan's schemes. Let's turn our attention to that conversation next.

TUNING IN | CHAPTER 6
Respond

1. What does the negative-self-talk energy drain typically entail for you? In other words, after you've entertained self-condemning thoughts for a while, how do you usually feel?

2. Which of the following promises from God speaks most profoundly to you, and why?

- "I have plans for you to prosper and succeed" (see Jer. 29:11).
- "I will carry your burdens for you and give you rest" (see Matt. 11:28–29).
- "I will meet all your needs" (see Phil. 4:19).
- "I will give you peace every day" (see John 14:27).

3. I mentioned that when Christ is set apart as Lord, other things can't then be lord in our lives. What other things do you need Jesus to be Lord of today? A particular fear or insecurity, maybe? A stressful situation? A relationship that's causing you pain? Something else?

Reflect

In the last section of this chapter, I mentioned that as we learn to make positive agreements—self-talk statements that align with God's truth—we can "refuse to lower our heads when times get tough, choosing instead to listen up, look up, and lift our heads to God." Think on this promise for a few minutes, and then write down how your demeanor would change if you lived from this reality instead of accepting negative agreements.

Read On

Take time to meditate on Isaiah 55. What is God saying to you through these verses?

PART THREE

THE CONVERSATION
BETWEEN YOU
AND THE ENEMY

7

DIVISION UNTO DESTRUCTION

The will is a beast of burden. If God mounts it, it wishes and goes as God wills; if Satan mounts it, it wishes and goes as Satan wills; nor can it choose its rider ... the riders contend for its possession.

—Martin Luther

When I was a kid, my parents were really strict about movies. This wasn't a huge issue for me until I became a teenager. Peer pressure was a big factor during those years, and I wanted to see the same movies all my buddies were always talking about. But these were the very movies my parents vehemently disallowed. If I was going to be "cool" in conversations with my friends, the only option left for me, I figured, was deceit.

A specific memory comes to mind: me at fifteen and the release of a disallowed movie that my friends were headed off to see. I breezed through the kitchen at dinnertime, while my mom was occupied with things other than making eye contact with me, and I told her that my friends and I were going camping. My dad was in the living room and could hear everything I was saying, so technically I'd lied to them both. Inside I felt horrible, but at least I'd get to see the flick.

The next day my mom asked about our camping trip—where we'd stayed, how the woods were that night, what we'd eaten. She wasn't interrogating me; she was just being a mom. But she may as well have had a spotlight shining on me for the penetrating beam her questions proved to be. I was so jittery and internally ashamed that I could barely stay in the same room with her. I hedged my way through the excruciating exchange, saying little more than a string of monosyllabic replies, and then I darted out the door to go find my friends.

As I say, this whole deal went down when I was fifteen, the same age when I went forward at church to pray with leaders of our congregation and surrender my heart to Jesus. Full-on devotion and outright deceit were now strolling hand in hand through my heart. It was a perplexing season for me.

A few weeks after I'd spoken untruths to my mom—and my dad—about going camping when I was really at the movies with my buddies, I wandered into the living room and told her that my friends and I were planning to go see a movie that night, one that she and Dad would think was fine.

In actuality, my friends and I illegally purchased beer and then downed every last drop of it at the lake house of one of my friends' parents. As luck would have it, we ran out of beer partway through the night and decided to head into town to get more. As we all barreled into the grocery store, intent on hitting the beer aisle, I caught sight of my mom and dad, who were there to pick up milk. This was not going to end well, I felt sure.

Despite the brain fog I was experiencing from the alcohol I'd consumed, I assessed this unfortunate scene with astounding clarity and precision. I was supposed to be at a movie theater, innocently enjoying a film with my friends. Instead, for the past ninety minutes, I'd been at my buddy's house in the middle of nowhere, building a campfire and guzzling beer. And then there were the cigarettes. Oh, great: in addition to being just beyond tipsy, I also smelled like tobacco. My parents weren't fond of tobacco.

I shot up a prayer to heaven: *God! My parents can't see me like this!* And then I forced my friends toward the store's exit, whereupon we hightailed it out of there.

"COULD IT BE ... *SATAN?*"

Now, I have a question for you. Were those episodes of deceitfulness simply harmless manifestations of adolescence, or were they the work of some demonic force? If you're of a certain age, you may remember the *Saturday Night Live* skits of old, featuring Dana Carvey as the Church Lady. The character, Enid Strict, hosted a fictitious television program called *Church Chat*, and in her famously pious, holier-than-thou tone, she would interview high-profile celebrities and athletes, asking them about their lifestyles and work.

Inevitably her guest would admit to some sort of indulgence or sin streak, to which the Church Lady would mockingly blame the Devil. She'd then slickly condemn the sinner in the guest chair to eternal damnation and pain in wonderfully crafted sarcasm, which always elicited a big audience laugh. The skit stuck, and still today we love to make a caricature of evil's influence in the world by responding to our deviance with the explanation, "Could your problem really be … *Satan?*"

I'm not an alarmist who imagines stealthy demons behind every bush, but I dare say Ms. Strict was onto something with her assessment of how evil unfolds. You and I have a very real, very active enemy in this world, and his name is Satan. His desire is to break through our defenses like a missile seeking heat.

So whenever Satan sees us inching toward godliness, he reaches for his weapons. Whenever he sees us allowing the Holy Spirit access to our minds and hearts, he takes aim. Whenever he sees us activate our faith by responding to hatred with kindness or marshaling self-control when we feel entitled to rage, he fires. He's forever tempting us to go our own way, because it's typically along that self-paved path that we sin.

Notice here that I said *we* sin; the Devil can't *make* us do anything. The apostle James confirmed this fact. When talking about the progression of temptation toward sin, he said,

> The temptation to give in to evil comes from us and only us. We have no one to blame but the leering, seducing flare-up of our own lust. Lust gets pregnant, and has a baby: sin! Sin grows up to adulthood, and becomes a real killer. (James 1:14–15 THE MESSAGE)

It may be strong language, but it's dead-on. It can be lust for power or prowess, fortune or fame, sleazy movies or a twelve-pack of beer. That lust for fleshly satisfaction is what drives us to sin. Still, while Satan may not be able to dictate our actions, he sure cheers loudest when we screw up. When I used my words to deceive instead of being direct, in the battle for those moments, Satan won.

THE PLAN: STEAL, KILL, DESTROY

Satan, Scripture says, comes only to "steal and kill and destroy" (John 10:10), a plan he accomplishes by dividing unto destruction, with a pit stop at isolation somewhere in between. The progression works like this: First, the Enemy encourages us to think divisive thoughts, which disconnect us from God, while he simultaneously encourages us to use divisive language, which disconnects us from authentic community (those who love us, such as our parents and our spouses).

His goal here is to keep dividing us further and further until we're left isolated and on our own. It's like trying to keep dividing a cracker in half until all you're left with is a useless crumb. Satan loves it when we've been reduced to useless crumbs in our efforts to join God's work.

Next, once we're isolated from God and godly people, Satan makes a sport out of piling it on. Case in point: last night, a Sunday night, I caught myself ruminating on my life. I'm forty-nine years old and have a lot of friends, but over the past decade or so, I've been captivated by the idea of growing old with only other pastors of large churches as friends, people who have roles in life similar to mine. I want to brainstorm with them, dream with them, confess with them, and, in some instances, commiserate with them about the ins and outs of megachurch life.

But as I sat there mentally rattling off the names of the pastors I know, I realized that only a handful of them are my closest friends, true partners in ministry.

Within mere moments of hopping onto this train of thought, I sensed the Enemy nudging me toward outright despair. *You're never going to have a friend who "gets" the world you live in, Brady. You're going to die a lonely man.*

See? *Pile it on.* Satan is such a schmuck.

This isolation step is critical to Satan's plan because nothing is quite as deleterious to mind, body, or soul as being separated from that which gives life. Think of an inmate in solitary confinement who suffers from both bodily ailments—high blood pressure, immunosuppression tendencies, erratic sleep patterns, inflammation, etc.—and cognitive issues—such as memory loss, difficulty discerning reality from delusion, and the inability to sort out what time it is or to do simple math.

Along these lines, the BBC (British Broadcasting Corporation) published an article last year detailing the weird mental slippage a British hiker faced when she and her buddies accidentally wandered over the border separating Iraq from Iran and were arrested and incarcerated by Iranian troops. The soldiers thought the hikers were spies, and in order to curtail their ability to communicate with each other, the Iranians put each of them in individual solitary-confinement cells.

The article described how Sarah Shourd spent eight straight weeks in a cell with zero human interaction before she was released. Had she stayed any longer, she might have gone totally mad. "At one point, I heard someone screaming," Shourd reported, "and it wasn't until I felt the hands of one of the friendlier guards on my face, trying to revive me, that I realised the screams were my own."[1]

In the movie *Cast Away*,[2] Tom Hanks famously screamed too, after being stranded on an island and ostracized from civilization for enough time. He also named a volleyball "Wilson" and spoke to it as he would a close friend in an attempt to keep isolation from getting the best of him.

More recently I caught a preview of an upcoming episode of the History Channel's show *Alone*:[3] ten contestants are abandoned separately in the Vancouver Island wilderness in Canada, with nothing but the packs on their backs, to see who can survive the longest with no partner, no producer, no cameraman, no host, no nothing. It was evident, even from the short clips, that those guys were unraveling too.

The upcoming episode centered on a downpour of magnificent proportions. Most people find a rain shower refreshing, but when you've been living in the woods by yourself for a month, scavenging for every meal, desperate for clean drinking water, and terrified out of your mind that the cougar you spotted last night is hot on your trail, the rainstorm that is destroying your makeshift shelter and drenching the handful of possessions you still can claim as your own can do you in.

Or what about the prophet Elijah? He wrestled with similarly debilitating thoughts. In 1 Kings 18–19, he had just put the god of King Ahab to the test, pitting Baal against Jehovah, the Lord of Hosts (if you haven't read the story, Baal got a 72–0 drubbing), and now Ahab and his wife, Jezebel, were irate. Elijah ran for his life, worried that they might make good on their threat that within twenty-four hours, they'd hunt Elijah down and kill him. Eventually he came to a shade tree and totally collapsed, exhausted from all the drama, exertion, and fear.

Not once but twice, an angel of God came to Elijah, shaking him awake, providing him with bread and water, and encouraging him to eat and then go back to sleep. But Elijah wouldn't be consoled. He'd been doing what God had asked him to do, working night and day to get the people of Israel to obey God, but he was sure his efforts had all been for naught. "I am the only [faithful] one left," he told God, "and now they are trying to kill me too" (19:10).

Elijah told God he just wanted to die. "'I have had enough, Lord,' he said. 'Take my life'" (v. 4). And with that, Satan surely smiled. *Yes! Division—check. Isolation—check. And now for the kill shot!*

Satan loves it when we buy into the idea that we're all alone in life, that nobody sees us and nobody cares, because it is then that we're like a bison calf separated from the herd. Suddenly we're easy prey for the lion stalking us from the brush. All that's left is the takedown.

A TOOTHLESS DRAGON

On Sunday mornings, just after I've finished preaching, from time to time I'll experience a fleeting series of thoughts that sound something like this: *That was awful. I'm sure nobody in this whole auditorium got anything out of that talk. Why am I even here? Why am I a pastor? I'm horrible at preaching. What in the world am I doing?*

To make matters worse, Satan then comes along and whispers something to this effect: *Yeah. You are pretty awful. You should go back to sports broadcasting and hang up the pastor role.*

The first few times this happened, the taunts were unnerving, but one afternoon when I was studying in the book of Revelation, I came across a familiar passage of Scripture that struck me in a totally fresh way, as though I'd never read it before: the apostle John, describing the scene involving the archangel Michael and his heavenly host fighting the great dragon (Satan), which culminated with the dragon and his evil angels being "hurled to the earth" (12:9). In the next verse, John named Satan "the accuser of our brothers and sisters," the one who "accuses them before our God day and night" (v. 10).

I stared at that description awhile, letting the words sink deep into my spirit. Satan—the guy who kept accusing me of being an awful preacher, teacher, and pastor—was going to be hurled down into the abyss in the end. One of the final acts of justice the world will ever know is when God's angels put Satan in his place. What's more, because of Christ's victory over sin—past, present, and future—this act of justice has already been secured. The actual event will happen in coming days, but we can rest in the finality of it *even now.*

This realization was a game changer for me. These days, whenever Satan saunters up to me as I'm descending the steps from the teaching platform to my front-row seat and whispers verbal venom in my ear, I silently whisper back to him, *You're going down in the end, Satan. Let the hurling begin.* Then I ask God to remind me of my identity, my calling, my equipping, and his love toward me, and I get after the work he has called me to do.

As an old preacher used to say, "Birds may fly over your head, but that's no reason to let them build a nest in your hair." Satan may bait us with his taunts, but we don't have to waste our time on them. We have more important things to do.

AVOIDING TEMPTATION AT ALL COSTS

The one and only time Jesus's disciples explicitly asked him to teach them something, it had to do with how to pray. In response Jesus proffered what we refer to as the Lord's Prayer, which is documented in two of the four Gospels—Matthew 6:9–13 and Luke 11:2–4. In both places an interesting appeal appears—that God would *lead us not into temptation*—and looking back on the seemingly benign childhood lies I told my parents about going camping and going to the movies, I totally understand why.

By the time I became an adult, I was lying about far more substantial things, including the illicit extracurricular activities I was engaged in during my college years and a secret porn habit I harbored shortly thereafter. I'd been practicing the art of deception for years. Lying was a piece of cake, which is exactly the point of that plea in the Lord's Prayer: Jesus knew that the more often we find ourselves in the clutches of temptation, the more often we fall into outright sin, and since sin is what distances us from God, we should avoid falling into temptation at all costs.

But how do we get that done?

Several months ago, our church hosted 150 men and women from all across the nation, all of whom serve as part of their churches' security teams. One of the beautiful by-products of the decidedly ugly turn of events that unfolded when a gunman drove onto our property that December 2007 morning has been a series of opportunities to help other churches improve the protection they afford their leaders and congregants. We learned a lot of lessons on the heels of that shooting, and there is a certain gratifying effect in being able to share those lessons with anyone who will listen and take them to heart. Hopefully our experience and what we learned from it will help others avoid a similar attack someplace else.

One of the key lessons we took away from that entire saga was that you can't underestimate the importance of spiritual discernment when it comes to securing your site. I explained to the men and women who gathered at our conference that on the morning of the shooting, the man who oversaw New Life's security team—a volunteer coordinator named Jeff Cowell—came into my office and said, "Pastor Brady, I called in some extra security teams today on a hunch that we might need those folks." There had been a shooting in the middle of the night an hour north of us at an unrelated ministry outpost, but because the shooter was still at large, Jeff decided to take extra precautions.

I would later learn that Jeff's "hunch" had come to him in a moment of prayer. Early that Sunday morning, he asked God for direction regarding how to protect our church's campus that day, and the answer was clear: *More people. More teams. Keep your eyes open today. Trouble is afoot.*

Looking back, I shudder to think what could have happened had Jeff not activated those additional armed guards. The shooter who penetrated our campus had more than one thousand rounds of ammunition on his person. One man's hunch, so many lives saved.

I told the security personnel at the conference that my greatest prayer for them was for the spiritual gift of discernment (see 1 Cor. 12:7–11)—that they would possess it in increased measure and pay attention to it in their hearts and minds. If they could learn to rightly discern the spirits, I said to them, they would not only know when the Enemy was encroaching, but they would also know where their heavenly Father was at work. They would know where they were vulnerable and where they were strong. They would have a heightened awareness of God's presence and anointing and be able to adjust their thoughts and actions according to his leading.

This is essentially what it means to avoid temptation: we distinguish the spirit of death from the spirit of life, the spirit of rebellion from the spirit of reverence, the spirit of degradation and self-absorption from the spirit of wholeness and holiness, the spirit of the Enemy from the Spirit of the One we serve.

It happens in the same way you instantly recognize the voice of your spouse, your mom, or a years-long friend when he or she calls. If you engage in frequent conversation with God, you'll know it's his voice when he calls, even before you check caller ID. You'll lean in to what he says and quickly go in the direction he's leading. You can then resist temptation at every turn.

WHEN WE KNOW BETTER, WE DO BETTER (SOMETIMES)

Along the way I've developed a shorthand method for deciding if the spirit of death or the spirit of life is influencing me in the words I'm about to speak. Let's suppose I'm having a conversation with someone, and I'm about to respond to what the other person just said. In the split second I have before I speak, I ask myself this question: *Will what I'm about to say unify or divide?*

If the answer is not clearly unify, then I don't say whatever I was going to say. (This approach would have served me well back when I was fifteen years old standing in the kitchen with my mom, a bald-faced lie on my lips. Lying definitely didn't unify anything for me. Instead, it divided mightily—my heart from hers and my heart from God's. I've tried to do better since then.) It always astounds me that such a simple question also has the power to keep my foot out of my mouth. Let me share an example from everyday life.

My family and I are terrible dog owners. I'm not sure why. Every cat we get thrives, but the dogs? We were zero for four when Callie began hinting that she wanted a new dog. For this reason I balked and reminded her of our track record, emphasizing in my little speech that *numbers don't lie*. But she was having nothing to do with my reasoning and rationale. "I'll buy it with my own money and take care of it myself, I promise," she said plainly. I told her we would think about it—my way of tabling the discussion in the hope that everyone would forget about it.

That was on a Tuesday. Three days later I left town to speak at a church a few states over, returning home late Sunday night. When I arrived home, my wide-smiling wife and wider-smiling daughter introduced me to Fia, the seventy-pound husky now living in our home.

"Her name is short for *Sofia*, Dad," Callie said. "Isn't that cute?"

Cute is not the word I was silently using to describe this turn of events. Nothing about this situation was *cute*. If a decision is going to affect all of us, we make that decision *together*—this is an unspoken and yet undeniable Boyd house rule. Here's another one: at all times there must be fewer pets than people in our household, a family rule this "*Fia* is short for *Sofia*" beast of burden had broken by her mere presence. And another rule: Pam and I don't go behind each other's backs and do things, *especially* things resulting in adding one more mouth to feed into the mix.

Internally a storm was brewing. I was tired from my trip, I was hungry after having missed dinner, and now this: the Boyd women had instigated a mutiny. My talking points began falling into line, dutiful soldiers armed and ready to fight. I was fully justified in my outrage, and I fully planned to give Pam and Callie a piece of my perturbed mind. And if Fia had a lick of sense in those husky bones, she would flee the scene immediately. Her days were numbered.

"We wanted to surprise you," Pam said, as if they had made me a cake or my favorite cookies. "And Callie has assured me she will take complete ownership of Fia's care—walking her, feeding her, bathing her, tending to whatever needs she has."

This was a setup. I was being had. And yet for reasons that are still unknown to me, my defenses softened. I began to rationalize: Did I wish I had been consulted about the purchase? *Of course.* Could I have done without their well-meaning "surprise"? *Most definitely.* But the event wasn't as big as I was making it—at some point we would have gotten the dog. To freak out over the issue of timing would have robbed my daughter of something important, which in this case was the celebration of her desire to care for a creature all on her own.

More important than any of that, though, was the real-time realization that if I had moved from being *tempted* to misuse my words to *actually* misusing them, I would have set into motion a whole awful chain of events that night, none of which would have honored God—or would have been any fun for anyone else, for that matter. Had I lashed out at Pam and shamed Callie, my relationship with both of them would have taken a hit. The next morning would have been awkward with one another, at best, and the subtle leaning away from one another instead of into each other would have had a lingering, detrimental effect. And guess who would have been overjoyed by that turn of events?

I looked at elated Pam and joyful Callie and simply said, "Fia's great. I'm happy for you. Now, let's talk guidelines, okay?" And we did. We agreed to the parameters of Fia's existence and hugged on it before heading to bed. Those boundaries were debased within forty-eight hours of being established, I should mention, which is when I had to shell out three hundred bucks upon discovering that Fia had eaten poop from the cats' litter box, resulting in her contracting a near-fatal condition and requiring several crazy-high-priced canine meds. But still … Callie meant what she said: this was her dog, and she'd do the hard work of seeing to it that Fia was walked and fed.

What I experienced that night was a tiny but satisfying taste of standing firm against the schemes of Satan. I had been communing with God the entire time I'd been ministering out of town. I was consequently refreshed in my confidence that I am embraced and empowered and loved. Because of that, when I was faced with the alluring temptation to power up over my wife and child, I was able to gracefully stand down instead.

Jesus, of course, was the master of triumphing over temptation. Think back on the triad of temptations he faced in the wilderness and how he overcame them, three for three. At the beginning of Jesus's ministry, Luke 4:1 tells us, "Jesus, full of the Holy Spirit, left the Jordan and was led by the Spirit into the wilderness." (To clarify, the S in Spirit is capitalized, which means this was the Holy Spirit leading Jesus, not an evil spirit.) There in the wilderness, Jesus underwent forty days of divinely appointed testing, but because he was rock-solid sure of who God was and rock-solid sure of who he was in light of God's presence and power in him, he prevailed.

To Satan's temptation that Jesus turn a stone into a loaf of bread and thus satisfy the hunger he surely felt forty days into his fast, Jesus said, "It takes more than bread to really live" (v. 4 THE MESSAGE). To Satan's temptation that Jesus worship Satan in exchange for dominion over all the kingdoms of the earth, Jesus said, "Worship the Lord your God and only the Lord your God. Serve him with absolute single-heartedness" (v. 8 THE MESSAGE). To Satan's temptation that Jesus challenge God's care by skydiving from the top of the temple and trusting the angels to break his fall, Jesus said, "Don't you dare tempt the Lord your God" (v. 12 THE MESSAGE).

The lust of the flesh, the lust of the eyes, and the pride of life—the temptations Satan tried on Jesus in Luke 4—are the identical ones he trots out for us today. Satan knew that if he could get Jesus to manifest self-importance, arrogance, and pride—the sense that he could be happy only if he had one more material possession, one more ounce of power, one more attaboy—then he could win Jesus to his side.

But Jesus could not be swayed, proving once and for all that when you relish constant conversation with God and allow his truth to saturate your thoughts, any temptation away from godliness only causes everything in you to rise up and say, "Nope. Not me. Not here. Not ever." Jesus's example shows us that a rock-solid relationship with our heavenly Father makes it really, really difficult to entertain a lifestyle of sin.

James 1:14 tells us, "Each person is tempted when they are dragged away by their own evil desire and enticed," which is imagery I really like. When you're doing life with God, to sin, you have to *really* want to sin. You have to literally be "dragged away" to fall into this kind of error. And yet, as we'll see in the next chapter, we find it all too easy to get dragged away sometimes.

TUNING IN | CHAPTER 7
Respond

1. When have you encountered a battle that seemed spiritual in nature, a time when you were endeavoring to make a God-honoring decision but were opposed, or a time when you walked headlong into a situation that you knew would not end well? Did you attribute the situation to the work of Satan? Why or why not?

2. What effects of isolation have you known? Do you agree or disagree with the idea that a big part of Satan's strategy to destroy us is to isolate us?

3. When have you been tempted to respond poorly to something someone said, and how did you handle it? What factors played

into your decision regarding how to respond? What forces do you believe are at work as you communicate with people throughout each day?

Reflect

When have you known better but not done better? Think about the situation—how you acted, what the results were, and what, if anything, you would do differently if you could replay the scenario and try again.

Read On

Scan the verses from 1 Kings 19, meditating on the strength of emotion Elijah—and God—expressed. What fresh perspective or new awareness can you take away from this encounter that can help you fend off hopelessness in your own life?

8

JUMPING THE FENCE

God's truth judges created things out of love, and
Satan's truth judges them out of envy and hatred.
—Dietrich Bonhoeffer, *Ethics*

I've always been something of a gunslinger with words, always locked and loaded and ready to fire—the kind of guy who is forever popping off a few rounds before so much as asking the other person's name. This approach to communication served me well as a kid growing up in the backwoods of Louisiana, with little more to talk to than the horse I rode bareback and the snakes I shot while barreling through. I was my own entertainment, chatting up the swamps, the sunset, the sky—anything and everything that provided the listening backdrop to my life.

Later, after I'd charmed my way through high school, college, and a parade of girlfriends, my ready-fire-aim rhythm landed me a job in sports broadcasting, where gunslingers congregate en masse. There's no greater liability in that particular profession than finding oneself at a loss for words, which is why, I assume, I was promoted quickly through the ranks. I *always* had something to say, and with nobody in particular on the receiving end of my color commentary, that "something" was entertaining, enlighten-ing, and spot-on—in my quick-fire estimation, at least.

During those early broadcasting successes, however, at least one person wasn't especially taken with my steamrolling style. Pam and I hadn't been married very long when I tried yet again (and unsuccessfully) to get her to tell me how she was feeling about things by using myself as the conversational gold standard. "Pam, you *never* have to wonder what I'm thinking or how I'm feeling!" I pointed out. "I always tell you *everything* that's on my mind!"

To which she replied, "Brady, sometimes a little mystery would be nice."

Huh? Now that was something I'd never considered before.

Years after that little exchange, I found myself pastoring a small church in West Texas, despite my earnest protests against God lead-ing me into full-time ministry. There again I was confronted with the fact that while being a somewhat entertaining, quick-witted chatterbox who rarely thought it necessary to weigh my words, over time I picked up on a distinctive vibe: it was all a little *much*. More specifically, *I* was a little much—a little *too* much.

I was a young guy surrounded by older, more seasoned men, and the way I coped with my feelings of inadequacy was to keep talking until I said something, as coach Lou Holtz once observed in a TV interview. I'd be in meetings and would just rattle off line after line until something clever or insightful or timely came out. I was pretty immature in my faith, but instinctively I knew I'd be better off being quiet and having these men suspect I was a fool rather than keeping my mouth open and removing all doubt—I just never did it (see Prov. 17:28).

In the decades to follow, friends and loved ones would inform me that I could be not just hypercommunicative but abrasive, impulsive, hasty, offensive, opinionated, and even, on especially talkative days, downright crude as well. It was never my intention, of course, to hurt people's feelings with my words, but given the truisms about how talking too much leads to sin, and how sensible people keep their mouths shut (see Prov. 10:19, for instance), this overtalker was bound to slip up more than those who were more measured and self-controlled. As it relates to Satan's strategies for me, I would make things far too easy for him.

A WORD TO THE WISE

The problems I had reining in my words as a young man stemmed from the fact that I wasn't entirely sure how to steward the communication gifts I'd been given. I'm comfortable speaking off the cuff, I love a fiery debate, and I can organize thoughts and convey them with words at a lightning-fast rate. I considered these things assets, even as my relationships were suffering as a result. As I look back on many of my exchanges with friends, colleagues, even my own wife, I can see the Enemy's fingerprints all over them. For instance, Pam and I would be in a tiff about something, and I'd just *bury* her with swift logic and skill. I was always circumspect about celebrating those victories—is winning an argument with your wife worth it if it means losing her heart?—but something needed to change, and I had a feeling that something was me.

Not wanting to blow up my marriage or drive away close friends, I began to pay attention to how wise people used their words. As I mentioned previously, I was surrounded by sages at that church in West Texas, and so, knowing I needed to shift gears in terms of how I communicated, I abandoned my goal of trying to impress with my quick wit and instead went to school on their communication style.

James 3 compares the tongue to a bit in a horse's mouth, which makes the giant animal turn whichever way the bit is pulled. The tongue is also like the tiny rudder of a ship that, even when strong winds are driving the ship, steers the craft at the pilot's whim. Finally James compared the tongue to a fire that can light up an entire forest. He warned that the tongue can be outright evil and "full of deadly poison" (v. 8). The men I was trying to learn from seemed to understand these things—namely, that if Satan could get our tongues wagging, we'd spew that "deadly poison" all over everyone.

They were also so faithful in honoring exhortations from Proverbs that I wondered if they'd memorized the entire book. It seemed second nature for them to exemplify sayings like these:

- "The one who has knowledge uses words with restraint, and whoever has understanding is even-tempered" (Prov. 17:27).
- "Those who guard their lips preserve their lives, but those who speak rashly will come to ruin" (13:3).
- "The heart of the righteous weighs its answers, but the mouth of the wicked gushes evil" (15:28).

These guys never, ever gushed. They were convinced at some meaningful level that God's communication guidelines were meant not to constrain them but to help them soar. Over time I'd come to the same conclusion: relational freedom is found *inside*, not outside, the fences God asks us to reside within.

THE PROTECTIVE PERIMETER GOD SETS

Learning to live well within the fences of protection God has put in place around us—fences that Satan, of course, abhors—matters to all of life. Invest a few intentional hours reading God's Word, and you'll discover a divinely placed sexual fence that says, "Wait until you're married to have sex; and then, once you've taken a spouse, have sex only with that person." Stepping outside that fence does us no favors, as far too many of us can attest. It's a move that actually *destroys* something valuable in us, according to Proverbs 6:32: "A man who commits adultery has no sense; whoever does so destroys himself."

There is a financial fence that says, "Don't go into debt. Plan for your expenditures, and then shop for a fair price." We in North America hate that fence and collectively bust through it all the time. Our government's spending patterns ought to serve as a cautionary tale: at the end of the last fiscal year (2015), we as a nation were sixteen and a half trillion dollars in debt. That's 16.5 with *twelve* places after it—that's a million million! Fences, people, *fences*.

There is also a relational fence that says, "Consider others' needs first. Practice humility. Don't elbow your way to the front of the line." And a vocational fence that says, "Do your work as though God were your boss." And an attitudinal fence: "Don't lose heart. Always keep hope alive." And a moderation fence: "Don't be a glutton—let a single glass of wine or serving of fries be enough." Fence after fence, the Bible lays out for us, posts and rails intended for our protection, boundary markers corralling us toward the heart of God. And *all* of them are profitable to acknowledge, understand, and respect. But perhaps none is more important to yield to than the fence that outlines God-honoring words.

The most concentrated advice on how to communicate well shows up in Ephesians 4. We're told there to "put off falsehood and speak truthfully … for we are all members of one body" (v. 25), and we're also advised, "In your anger do not sin" (v. 26). We're told not to "let any unwholesome talk come out of your mouths, but only what is helpful for building others up according to their needs, that it may benefit those who listen" (v. 29). And we're instructed not to "grieve the Holy Spirit of God, with whom you were sealed for the day of redemption" (v. 30).

The apostle Paul ended his spiel by packing the biggest punch: "Get rid of all bitterness, rage and anger, brawling and slander, along with every form of malice. Be kind and compassionate to one another, forgiving each other, just as in Christ God forgave you" (vv. 31–32). When we use our words the way God asks us to use them, Paul essentially says, we can speak life and peace and joy to others. When we don't use them well, we speak chaos and death, revealing that once again we've jumped the fence. Satan must cheer every time.

The funny thing about that Ephesians passage is that as rational people we say, "Yeah, that all sounds good," even as we fail to implement it in our own lives. What we really mean when we nod our heads in agreement with Paul's words is, "Yeah! That's exactly how people should talk *to me*."

Therein lies the rub: we're not asked to help keep everyone else within the fences of God's commands; we're asked to keep *ourselves* there—preferably every day. If we do so, we'll know relational freedom as we've never known it before; if we don't, we won't. It all comes down to what we do with exhortations like those in Ephesians 4. Will we choose to get rid of bitterness? Will we choose to put away lies? Will we forgive as Jesus has forgiven us? Will we choose to build others up rather than tear them down?

The alternative is a straightforward one: if we refuse to live within God's protective perimeter, we become more vulnerable to Satan's schemes. That vulnerability inevitably leads to our sinning more frequently, which only increases the distance between us and God. And when we're doing life at arm's length (or farther!) from God, it's impossible to reflect the character traits that only intimacy with him can yield.

From reading this I hope you're making the connection that the only way we can actually be honest and forgiving, compassionate and wise, is if we allow our heavenly Father to empower us, letting his input run our lives. By this point in this book, you're now probably gathering what that divine direction should sound like:

"Get rid of your bitterness. Really. Be kind."

"Stop fighting. Be helpful with your words."

"Anger is doing you no favors. Let it go. Give grace instead."

(And if you aren't, I would suggest reviewing part 1 again and getting a refresher on hearing from heaven through reading and meditating on God's Word.)

METHINKS THOU DOTH PROTEST ...

There are several ways we jump the fences God has lovingly built for us as it relates to how we use our words. The good news is that if we've strayed beyond those borders, we can choose to do an about-face and come home. (And we all know what it's like when we *have* strayed beyond those borders, yes?)

But before we dive into those missteps, I'd like to offer a word of encouragement. If you're the type of person who is teachable and humble of spirit, you'll probably spot yourself in one of the following not-so-pleasant categories and immediately feel remorse. You'll hear the evil whispers of Satan that tell you you've always been a loser, you'll always be a loser, and a loser's all you are today, and you'll believe them down to your toes. What I want to say to you is this: it's okay. Really, *it's okay*. Forgiveness is waiting for you within the fence, and it's never too late to come back.

If, on the other hand, you're the type of person who can't for the life of you imagine that your communication patterns could be painted in a negative light, then I would simply ask you to consider which of the categories lights you up. Very possibly, it's that same communication tendency others see in you.

Let me show you what I mean.

Recently I became so frustrated when a guy at Starbucks blew me off that I decided to document my top-ten list of annoyances about the species known as humankind. This has to be one of

Satan's favorite ploys, by the way, as part of his mission to stoke our pride. He gets us to focus with laserlike attention on everyone else's irritating traits so that we no longer see or address our own. But back to the Starbucks guy: Can I rant for a couple of pages? It might just enhance your life.

> **10.** I'm annoyed by people who constantly wear a Bluetooth ear fob that is so microscopic you can't tell it's there. The reason this is annoying is that when I walk by such people and offer a friendly "Hello!" they say something in response that's not directed at me. (I'm looking at you, Starbucks Dude!) I can't tell you how many times this has happened to me. I'll say "Hello!" and they'll say, "I *need* those figures, Jack," while giving me that certain look that says, "You moron. Don't you see the very important device in my ear?" And then I'll mutter unkind things under my breath in response.

> **9.** I'm annoyed when people text someone else while they're having a conversation with me. I might have to poke my eyes out if I work through the latest example of this awful trend, so I think I'll just leave it at that. Surely you've experienced what I'm talking about.

> **8.** I'm annoyed when people forget to silence their phones before church services. Also in this

category: people who don't know how to silence their ringing phones immediately by simply pressing the down-volume button on the phone's side, and instead fumble with it for five minutes without being able to figure out how to make it quiet.

7. I'm annoyed by school fund-raisers. (This isn't technically a "people" category, but I needed to get it off my chest.) I can't tell you how much average cookie dough and bad popcorn I've eaten over the years just to be nice to a cute, polite kid. One word: *annoying*.

6. I'm annoyed when slow drivers hang out in the passing lane. Hello? Any idea what the right lane is for?

5. I'm annoyed when people repetitively tap, click, or smack things. If you have a pen in your hand and are constantly clicking it—*flick, flick, flick, flick*—then for the sake of sanity humankind-wide, please, please, please put the thing away and leave it alone. Same goes for popping gum, tapping fingernails on the table, and cracking knuckles. Just—*stop*.

(This is feeling so good, I have to tell you.)

4. Okay, I'm annoyed by people with coffee breath. If this is you, I have a word from the Lord for you: *Altoids.*

3. I'm annoyed when parents count to their children, as in, "Billy, you'd better stop that! One! ... Two! ... Two and a half ... Two and three-quarters ..." Parents, this approach doesn't work. Does your boss count for you before he or she expects compliance? I didn't think so. Ask once, and if your kids don't obey, spank their rear ends and be done with it. (Save your emails. The Bible covers me here.)

2. I'm annoyed when people take up two parking spaces with their puny compact cars. There are two simple ways to avoid this: (1) *practice*, or (2) *assess*. When you get out of your car, just give a little glance. Are your wheels between the bright white lines?

And (drum roll, please ...)

1. I'm annoyed by guys who wear skinny jeans (which unfortunately includes many of my staff members at New Life). My advice to you all: the next time you go shopping, check out the *men's department* for a change.

I'm just saying: if you get to the gossip section in what follows
and find yourself all amped up, maybe take a passing glance in a
mirror. While Satan might be telling you that you're justified in
spewing smut, the Lord could be talking to you too (just as he
is to me right now about my top-ten list of annoyances), and if
you choose to listen, your life will get better. Please hear me on
this: stepping off the world's path and back onto the protected
field of God's system will bring joy to your soul and life to every
relationship you have. And the good stuff doesn't end there. When
you accept God's directives for how to use your words, you'll help
others find freedom as well.

I meet way too many people who've been burned by the
church somewhere along the way, and it always traces back to
words. They shared a struggle with a professing Christian in hopes
of being encouraged or prayed for or accompanied in the hunt for
resources that would alleviate some of their pain, and in response,
they got betrayed. The Christian shared their struggle with some
third party, and now, in addition to dealing with the original issue,
they bear the burden of a sullied reputation.

As you'll remember from the previous chapter, when we shame
others like this, we play right into Satan's divisive game. The people we shame then isolate and insulate until that particular storm
passes, and then they resolve to never open up to a Christian again.
"That was far too painful," they tell themselves. "I've learned my
lesson." Then they return to a world of darkness, determined to
steer clear of people of the Light from there on out. And of course,
we "shoot" and wound other Christians—astoundingly, this happens among believers as well.

But of course the inverse is also true: when we sign up for going God's way—remember Ephesians 4?—and choose to be careful with our words, we can *draw* people to Jesus's side. By modeling compassion, encouragement, and grace, we can teach them how to strengthen their relational ties. But first, we must set up shop on God's side of the fence, and then we must refuse to keep going AWOL.

THE WAYS WE GO AWOL

I want to say at the outset that I acknowledge we live in a fallen world surrounded by fallen individuals, with you and me counted among them. So please don't read into the following categories that I'm expecting perfection from anyone. Relational harmony and wholeness aren't possible every hour of every day, but I hope you agree we can get better at using our words to build up instead of tear apart. "Incidental contact" will happen from time to time— what we *can't* tolerate are flagrant fouls. Deliberate divisiveness gives Satan an upper hand he doesn't deserve and squelches God's good work in and through our lives.

Second, I want to offer a quick piece of advice should you find yourself battling in one of the areas we're about to cover: *close your mouth*. What is stored up in your heart is *going to come out*, so if what you've stored up isn't positive, close your mouth. Jesus described it this way in Matthew 12:33: "Make a tree good and its fruit will be good, or make a tree bad and its fruit will be bad, for a tree is recognized by its fruit." Wait until you have the chance to swap out anger for grace, but for now—*really*—the pie hole ought to be shut.

Now, to the fence jumps we want to watch out for.

Grumbling

Of all the flagrant communication fouls, the one that shows up most often is *grumbling*. This makes sense to me because it's *just so easy* to grumble. Sometimes when I'm stuck in traffic, I pass time watching how the people around me are responding. A few weeks ago we had unexpected cold weather here in Colorado as a rogue springtime snowstorm blew through our region, leaving behind piles of ice, hail, and snow where clean, passable roads had once been. Cars were sliding all over the place, which meant that drivers were highly stressed, since Colorado drivers usually know how to drive when it's icy and snowy out.

I noticed that people did different things in response to that stress. Some let the stress get to them. Another driver would inadvertently slide into their lane, and they made all sorts of unkind hand gestures while angrily shouting things no one else could hear. I don't think they had any idea how funny they looked. It was like a slapstick silent movie.

Other people didn't react that way at all. They approached the situation with a level head: the weather was deteriorating, the conditions were beyond anyone's control, and we were all just doing the best we could out there while trying to get home where it was warm and safe.

Two of the pastors on our staff were trying to get back to the church after a meeting they'd had on the west side of town that night, and they later told me that as they neared the interstate, they came over a hill where lots of cars were either stuck or sliding uncontrollably in directions they didn't mean to go. My friends rolled to a stop to assess the situation, which is when they made out a figure in the falling snow. There, in the middle of the inter-section, with snow-covered cars veering this way and that, was a man in a winter coat directing traffic.

My two friends got a closer look and realized that they knew the good Samaritan, who was risking life and limb to help people in need. It was a twenty-something guy who is part of our church community and is training to be an EMT (emergency medical technician). He had come upon the same scene an hour earlier, and instead of getting annoyed or rushing away from there toward self-preservation, he parked his car in a safe place, climbed across the shallow ditch on the south side of the road, and got busy triag-ing needs. His whole mind-set was, "How can I help? What can I do?" Now that's a rare approach.

My grandmother used to tell me that you can always tell what's inside people by bumping them. When you do, what's in them is what comes out. It's true. You and I walk around with our cups full of something, and when we get bumped, what spills out is who we are. If you've filled your cup with gentleness, compassion, and a spirit of service, kindness, and joy—all resources found in abun-dance *inside* the fences God has built—then when aggravations come along and bump you a little, what pours out of you will be beautiful and sweet.

If, on the other hand, what you've filled your cup with is bit-terness, self-centeredness, rejection, hatred, and pain—outside-fence realities that the Enemy promotes—then I guarantee what will spill out when you're bumped will be irrational and vile.

As I made my way home that snowy afternoon, I thought about how I'd spent the previous two hours in my office studying for a sermon I planned to give the following Sunday morning. I'm not always a man of contentedness and peace, but that day I felt soulishly at rest. My spirit was calm and relaxed. So what came out of me when the weather "bumped" me was a sense of unity with these fellow drivers, and the realization that we were collectively in harm's way. Nothing in me wanted to yell at anyone or grumble about my lane being *mine*. Mostly I just felt concern that we all got home safe and sound.

Of all Jesus's friends, the apostle Peter would probably have been given the title Biggest Loudmouth, and yet it was Peter who touted the benefits of holding one's tongue. "The end of all things is near," he wrote,

> therefore be alert and of sober mind so that you may pray. Above all, love each other deeply, because love covers over a multitude of sins. Offer hospitality to one another without grumbling. Each of you should use whatever gift you have received to serve others, as faithful stewards of God's grace in its various forms. If anyone speaks, they should do so as one who speaks the very words of God. (1 Pet. 4:7–11)

I like how Peter made a direct connection between going through life without grumbling and remembering to love each other well. In my experience I can't both grumble and love well at the same time. If I'm grumbling, I'm revealing to the watching world that something is broken in my heart or that I'm being influenced by the Enemy. I'm hurt, and I'm choosing to see the world through the lens of that pain.

Here Peter said, "See the world through the lens of love instead."

Oh, this is funny. As irony would have it, as I'm sitting here at my computer typing up a section on the adverse consequences of grumbling, I've just received an email from one of the chronic grumblers in my life. I was expecting to hear from her soon, but the fact that her note came in right now is amusing. The reason I thought she'd reach out is that she is on our staff and oversees a group for which I just made a policy shift. I knew she wouldn't be fond of the new policy, and because I hear from her only when something I've done dissatisfies her, I figured I'd be on her call list this week.

The policy centers on the kinds of people who are "allowed" to be volunteers at our church. While we want to find service opportunities for anyone and everyone who wishes to serve, we have to take precautions so that we don't put anyone in a compromising situation. For example, if someone has just been paroled after serving time for sexually predatory behavior, we have to be supercareful where we invite that person to serve. On the flip side, though, the fact that someone is choosing to make moral decisions that the Bible frowns upon doesn't necessarily mean that person cannot and should not serve in the local church, which is what my recent policy shift addressed.

I told this particular ministry that people who are still sorting out their walks with Christ (aren't we all!) and what "full surrender" would look like in their lives must be allowed to serve in appropriate ways, even in the most vital ministries of our church. Granted, if a person hasn't yet decided to surrender his or her life to Christ, that person probably shouldn't be discipling other people, but could he or she volunteer on the team that sets up tables before ministry meetings or the team that makes follow-up calls to people who indicate interest in a particular event—especially under the supervision of a more mature and devoted follower of Christ? Of course. Or at least I thought this should be the case. My entire senior staff agreed, and so we approved a shift in policy that called for this to happen. I know at least one person disagreed with our decision, the person I just heard from.

So now that I've written about the grumbler, a second dose of irony hits me as I tap away on my keyboard: By grumbling about the grumbler, what does that make me? See, without God's grace we're *all* doomed to toxic thoughts and communication. We're all doomed to giving Satan the short-term win.

The thing with chronic grumblers is that all of life appears to them as either black or white—gray doesn't exist. But this isn't how Jesus approached the world. If you think about it, Jesus should have been the biggest grumbler ever to live. He came from heaven, where everything is perfect, and entered planet Earth, where everything is not. The Bible could have been full of complaints and gripes, and Jesus would have been totally justified in every instance. But it's not, for the simple reason that Jesus didn't see a black-or-white world. He saw the world—and all of humankind—as a nuanced, complex, highly intriguing organism in need of deep compassion and unparalleled love. In short, when he looks at people and life and the situations we all face from time to time, he doesn't see those *liberals*, those *women*, those *blacks*, those *gays*, those *whatever*. He sees souls. He sees people he came to save.

First Peter 4:9 says that lovers of God should "offer hospitality to one another without grumbling," which ought to be instructive to you and me both. "If anyone speaks," Peter continued two verses later, "they should do so as one who speaks the very words of God."

Instead we say,

"This awful weather!"

"That waste-of-time sales meeting!"

"This stupid new policy!"

"Those Republicans!"

"Those Democrats!"

"Old people!"

"Today's youth!"

"Idiots with Bluetooth devices implanted permanently in their ears!"

(Oops. Does any of this sound like grumble-free hospitality to you?)

Suffice it to say, you and I probably both have room for some growth in this area. Let's move on.

Harsh Words

A woman Pam and I have been friends with ever since moving to Colorado nearly a decade ago has an interesting quirk. We all have idiosyncrasies, but over the past few years as I've been on this journey toward measuring my words more carefully, her quirk has really stood out to me. She is a fun person with a heart of gold, but she has a habit of rebuking me in a passive-aggressive way for being "too politically correct" whenever I preach.

We both laugh about it, and sometimes I give her a hard time about it, but she'll say things like, "I bet we'd see a lot more people give their lives to Christ if our church shot straighter on what is *right* and what is *wrong*." Other times she'll be direct and to the point: "Quit shying away from the truth, Brady! Give 'em both barrels!"

The last time she used the "Give 'em both barrels!" line, I cringed inside. All I could think was, *She wants me to be a gunslinger again, but that doesn't work. I know from experience! That's not my goal at all.* Unwittingly she was asking me to return to the person I've been trying for years to leave behind. She wanted me to tell people "how it is." She wanted me to shame people who didn't see things from my point of view.

Without realizing it, she was encouraging me to surrender to the Enemy's divisive schemes. She wanted me to come locked and loaded on Sunday mornings and hit people between the eyes with "truth." I can't fault her, really. We live in a spectacle-hungry society where people prize the "Gotcha!" immeasurably more than grace. And nobody's better than a gunslinger at dishing up a show.

This is why down through the ages certain politicians have attracted so much attention. They're slick, they're quick, they're as entertaining as the day is long. And they have *zero* fear about saying what they're thinking, regardless of whether that articulation will be useful, timely, or wise. Every book is written in a season of time. I'm writing this one in the spring of 2016 as the presidential debates and primaries are raging. Recently my kids and I were watching one of the presidential debates, and in response to the wildly irresponsible use of words and the total lack of humanity in nearly all of the candidates' communications, Abram and Callie looked at me, snarling with repulsion.

"Who *talks* like that?" Abram asked, an indication that while Pam and I are far from perfect parents, at least our kids know cruelty when they see it—or hear it, as the case may be. Still, while this degrading level of discourse totally turned us off, none of us turned off the TV. The use of harsh words—sarcasm, cursing, put-downs, vile jokes, and more—is wickedly pleasurable to watch, which is why we as a species keep it around. Yet its effects are undeniably corrupt. It harms everyone it hits. And Satan is right there in the middle of it all, cheering as the poison pours out of our mouths.

It's good that we remember Ephesians 4:29: "Do not let any unwholesome talk come out of your mouths, but only what is helpful for building others up according to their needs, that it may benefit those who listen." I think there's some wisdom in those words.

Gossip

Engaging in gossip isn't altogether different from my experience of eating too much fried catfish every single time I'm back in Louisiana. If you know anything about catfish, you know they're disgusting creatures. They're bottom-feeders that consider algae, insects, and leeches "fine dining." But if one of those suckers is caught, rolled in cornmeal, and fried up in near-rancid oil, without exaggerating, *I just can't get enough.*

Comfort food like no other, I tell you. It tastes so good and goes down so easily … but a few hours later, my innards begin to revolt. I search desperately for some way to get the effects out of my system. *Maybe a shower will help. Or a workout?* I think. *Yeah, I'll sweat it out.* But I soon realize my search is in vain. The toxicity is in my system now, and I'm just going to have to let it run its course.

Why do we do this to ourselves? Why, when we channel-surf past TMZ, do we have to flip back *just for a second* to see what's being said? Yes, it slides down easily. Right before it makes us sick.

We do this because in the moment, submission to Satan's instruction seems a better option than submission to God's. And we do this because inside every one of us lives a little bit of Salacious Crumb–like fascination with the perils other people face. Do you remember him, the yellow-eyed monkey-lizard from *Return of the Jedi*?

Salacious Crumb was the court jester for crime lord Jabba the Hutt and had a maniacal, cackling laugh you don't soon forget. The terms of Crumb's employment were straightforward: if the strange beast managed to amuse Jabba at least once daily, he would be allowed to stay and eat and drink as much as he wished. If he failed to do so, he would be killed. To accomplish his do-or-die goal, Crumb mocked anyone and everyone—except his boss, of course—doing virtually anything to get a laugh.

The part of him that resides in our sometimes-deceitful hearts is the part that cranes toward the salacious crumbs of another's misfortune or grief. Collectively, our self-esteem is very low, so when we hear someone quietly say, "You won't believe what she did …" even across a crowded room, we can't help but inch our way toward the gossipy morsel in the hope of learning something bad about someone else so that we can feel better about ourselves. We jump God's protective fence and gobble up the juicy morsels Satan tosses our way.

And despite our protests to the contrary, Christians can be the worst at this. We nod our heads in agreement that we gain good favor with God not by works of righteousness but by unmerited grace, even as we troll for ways to elevate ourselves by rolling around in the details of someone else's plight like a dog in the carcass of a dead skunk.

- "Well, if *he's* struggling with porn, then maybe this lust thing I'm wrestling with isn't really so bad after all."
- "Wow. *She* said *that?* I'm not as horrible a wife as I thought."
- "What? He got picked up on a DUI? I may drink a bottle of wine a night, but I would *never, ever* get a DUI."
- "I can't believe it. *He* was sleeping with *her* all along. Only a fool gets caught!"

Juicy morsels swept from the table of despair, but aren't we all prey to swallowing them, bite after delectable bite? *You're better than that!* Satan whispers. *Look what they did! Now you've got proof.*

Ah, but his isn't the only voice speaking. Lean in. Your Father is near.

You are my beloved, God says. *You are my prize. I have loved you with an everlasting love. You don't have to earn it; it's already yours.* And yet we keep on fighting for ways to prove that we're not as bad as the next guy, or the next gal.

No proof necessary whatsoever, God whispers, even as we turn to a friend and spread the smut.

It happened again today. I was having a normal conversation at Panera Bread with someone I know, and then without any notice, he took a hard left turn, no clutch. Within seconds he had delved into chatter about a mutual friend of ours. "Hey, did you hear about …" was how it began. I felt my head shaking before I had a chance to process the fact that by shaking my head—and, in effect, answering his question—I was encouraging him to go on. I didn't want him to go on, but before I gathered my wits enough to discourage him, he'd continued.

Before I even realized it, the catfish was sliding down my throat again.

Gossip is two things: (1) sharing the right information with the wrong person and (2) sharing the wrong information with anyone. As the immediate details this man was sharing flooded my consciousness, I realized I was neither part of our mutual friend's problem nor part of his solution.

The information being passed to me had no business being shared. I held up my hand to stop my friend from going on, but it was too late. I already knew our mutual friend's situation— probably a situation he didn't want me to know. (If he wanted me to know, he would have told me himself, right?)

I thought back to the night before, when Pam and the kids and I were at our friends' house. They had just gotten a new puppy. All the kids were jostling the poor pooch around so much that after an hour or so, the overstimulated dog vomited all over Callie.

Callie came rushing downstairs to the basement where the adults were watching a ball game and said, "Dad, the dog just threw up all over me."

She wanted me to help her clean things up, but as I took her in, standing there with goo all over her shirt, I thought, *I'm not going to get out of this situation without also getting slimed.*

Satan's slimy tactics can tempt us to jump the fence into the dangerous territory of gossip if we're not careful.

So, can we please agree to three soul-saving steps as it relates to gossip's ways?

1. When someone comes to us with information that doesn't pertain to us, we will stop the discourse midconversation. If we're not part of the problem and we're not part of the solution, then we shouldn't be part of the flow of communication. It's as simple as simple can be.

2. After we've stopped the gossiper midconversation, we will send that person back to someone who can make things right.

3. And finally, if we've been guilty of gossip recently, we will call the ones we've told and say, "I'm so sorry I shared that with you. I shouldn't have opened my mouth."

Anger and Abuse

It's a scientific fact that when we become angry, the blood coursing through our bodies suddenly rushes to our heads. If you've ever gotten so mad that you felt the blood rush to your head, you weren't imagining things. What you were experiencing was *real* and perhaps more pervasive than you thought. As blood hits our cranial region, our listening literally shuts down. Our ears get so flushed with blood that we will not—actually *cannot*—hear. It's for this reason that whenever we engage in a heated argument, everything around us seems muted and dim.

Which is why, I presume, the apostle James promoted a clear slow-to-anger policy: "Everyone should be quick to listen, slow to speak and slow to become angry, because human anger does not produce the righteousness that God desires" (James 1:19–20). The more we listen and process as reasonable human beings, the more we'll defuse our reasons for being angry. But our Enemy doesn't want us to listen, so he tries to create as much mayhem as possible.

Unfortunately we don't always choose this course, which is when anger takes root and grows. And what anger grows into is always abominable and fierce, always vicious and abusive and cold. But it doesn't have to go this way. We don't have to be pawns in Satan's hands. God says, *Trust me. I've got your back.* If you're prone to anger, I want to encourage you to find your triggers and then steer clear of them. Don't let people push your buttons; instead, choose the righteousness and peace of God.

WHEN WE TEND TO FLEE
After the Holy Spirit led Jesus through the three temptations, Luke 4 tells us, "When the devil had finished all this tempting,

he left [Jesus] until an opportune time" (v. 13). This brings me to a critical point regarding Satan: he's a strategist through and through. He knows when we're hungry, exhausted, or dehydrated, or when we've been sitting in front of a computer for too long and are getting bored, and he chooses that moment—*right then*—to pounce. He chooses then to lure us over the fence.

I know stay-at-home dads and moms who have to be extraordinarily circumspect about the hours between 4:00 and 6:00 p.m. They've been alone in the presence of needy children all day long, and by that point they're *done*—d-o-n-e *done*. I know professionals who solve problems all day long, and by five o'clock they're ready to scream.

I've heard of women who have tried to initiate a big "discussion" with their husbands right before bed, and parents who have tried to reason with a cranky toddler who hasn't had his lunch, and college athletes who worked to psych themselves up for the big game while they were still recovering from the flu. To all of them I say, "Things will go much better if you'll meet the practical needs for rest, nutrition, and health *first* before you take on anything else."

My greatest point of vulnerability is weariness. I'm a pastor, which means I stand up in front of our church every Sunday morning and try to compel people to live for Christ. Because of the rhythm of my weeks, I have to be very aware of my self-talk on Saturday nights and again on Sunday morning before I preach. I also need to be wary of Sunday afternoons and evenings, just after giving every ounce of energy I had that morning. Why? Because the Enemy of my soul *loves* to infiltrate my thoughts with untruths when I'm exhausted, poured out, and spent.

My family and I recently returned from an extended vacation in Florida where we swam, boated, ate delicious food, spent too many hours in the bright, blazing sunshine, went on bike rides, and shared countless meaningful conversations unimpeded by the general distractions of home. It was a terrific time.

I was thinking about that vacation this morning, and how refueling it was for me on every front. During my weeks away I carved out time each day to think and pray. I practiced gratitude by telling my family, as often as I could remember, how much I love being with them. I exercised every day. I read excellent books that challenged my mind and inspired my heart. And I didn't turn to substances to self-medicate the general angst of life. Not surprisingly, given how full my tanks were, my self-talk during that vacation was marked by energy, enthusiasm, and truth.

Granted, I can't take a vacation fifty-two weeks out of the year. What I *can* do is more rigorously monitor my self-talk when I realize my tanks have gotten low, so I don't leave myself vulnerable to the Enemy. You can do the same. If you're hungry, let your words be few. If you're tired, let your words be few. If you're suffering from cabin fever, let your words be few until you get outside and the sun hits your face. Know your triggers and avoid them at all costs. Trust me, you'll make fewer mistakes that way.

STRONGER TOMORROW THAN WE ARE TODAY

In the previous chapter, we looked at the perilous by-products of being tempted, but I'd like to draw your attention to another of temptation's effects. While temptation can (and often does) lead us toward sinfulness, ("jumping the fence"), it can also provide strength for fighting the good fight. It can prove to us that we are overcomers and that we don't have to cave in to the Enemy's schemes. Think about it: Are you still saying yes to the same temptations you signed up for ten or twenty years ago? Or have you wised up a little since then?

Listen, twenty years ago I was a very angry person. (If you don't believe me, Pam will back me up on this.) Anger bubbled up in the depths of my heart and could erupt—*boom!*—just like that. But these days? I'm a man of peace. I'm stronger, I'm more mature, I'm more faithful in my walk with God. Sure, I still sin daily like the rest of humankind, but *anger?* It's no longer my gig.

As you know, my working hypothesis is that the more we engage lovingly with God, the more every other relational exchange improves. This means that I no longer fall for the same ludicrous lies Satan tries to dish up. When he comes after me now, my response is, *Seriously? That's the best you can do? You need a bigger weapon if you're planning to ever take me down.*

Sinfulness doesn't mesh with me anymore. I crave the peace and power of Christ! That's why I keep fighting for the better way to say something—the Jesus way, the "bless you" way—rather than giving in to my old tendencies. Thank God for his promise to make us new!

TUNING IN | CHAPTER 8
Respond

1. Which communication patterns from Ephesians 4 seem easier for you to abide by, and which seem more difficult? Scan the following list, putting a plus sign (+) beside descriptions that usually characterize your speech and a minus sign (–) beside the ones that often don't.

- Speak the truth in love.
- Say what will build others up.
- Speak without bitterness.
- Speak without rage.
- Avoid getting into verbal fights.
- Avoid gossip.
- Avoid hateful speech.
- Be kind and compassionate.
- Be quick to forgive.
- Speak words of life.

2. When you grumble, what do you tend to grumble about? What does your answer reveal about your posture toward God?

3. What role do harsh words play in your communication patterns?

4. How has being the subject of gossip hurt you? Given that gossip has stung all of us, do you still find it alluring? Why or why not?

5. What triggers your anger? What assumptions, experiences, or predispositions shape your feelings about the appropriateness of anger in a person's life?

6. When are you most vulnerable to jumping the fence—e.g., to playing into Satan's destructive plans for your life? What precautions might help you avoid such situations with greater frequency?

7. What do you hope tomorrow's strength will look like for you? In other words, which part of the fence do you hope never to jump again?

Reflect

Take a moment to ponder the truth that each time we speak an unkind word, we have in essence jumped God's fence. How does this assessment square with your understanding of how relationships work? What reservations (or outright protests) do you have about residing within the communications fencing that God has put in place?

Read On

Read Ephesians 4, making note of the one aspect of communication you'd like to make progress in.

9

WHAT FORGIVENESS ALWAYS ACHIEVES

Hate cannot drive out hate. Only love can do that.
—Martin Luther King Jr.

One night a couple of years ago, I was sitting on my back deck fuming. Nobody was out there but me, but I was having quite a conversation, *out loud*. It was a gorgeous Colorado night, complete with a full moon standing guard over the tops of the pines, reflecting a stunning glow over the entire Palmer Divide. There was no wind, which is unusual for this part of the country, just enough of an easy breeze to counteract the warmth of the summer night. The entire scene was made for peace, for quiet reflection, for deep-seated joy—and yet there I sat, fuming.

It started when I remembered that somebody I care about had wronged me earlier that week. In the same way that you're only reawakened to the fact that you have tendinitis in a wrist or elbow when you rotate the joint just so, I had happily gone on with my days that week, largely forgetting I was upset with that person, until something in my consciousness rotated just so, a subtle whisper from the Enemy caught my attention, and a surge of pain and anger coursed through my entire being. Tendinitis of the soul: that's what ruptured relationships feel like.

So the memory came back to mind—of his saying what he'd said, of my responding the way I'd responded, and of our ending the conversation on a sour note and leaving each other's company in a less-than-honorable way. So I fumed, audibly. I launched into an imaginary exchange with the person, spouting off corrections and rebuttals, explanations and demands. I always have the best responses *after* the fact, days after the actual exchange, and now I was really nailing him.

This went on for many minutes before I detected a still, small whisper in the back of my head—a whisper of a different sort. *Brady,* the voice said, *I'd love to have a conversation with you tonight, but I can't cut through the noise.*

Sometimes it doesn't take a spiritual giant to recognize the voice of God.

You're spending all this time having an imaginary conversation with someone who isn't even here, he continued, *while I'm here, just waiting, eager to talk with you.*

BUT WE DON'T *WANT* TO FORGIVE

So far we've looked at the beneficial by-products of staying connected conversationally to God (this was part 1 of the book), and how that singular practice sets into motion the powerful progression of being able to tether our self-talk to truth and, consequently, to then stand firm against Satan's schemes (parts 2 and 3, respectively). God's invitation to you and me is that if we'll prioritize hearing and responding to his voice, he will guide and direct us, provide for and protect us, instruct us and inform our words—and really, who in their right mind wouldn't want those things?

When the One who created you, who feels unfathomable love and grace toward you, and who is committed to your constant improvement is willing and able to pull up a chair and chat—any hour of any day—I think you'd agree that life is pretty good. Those conversations can't help but improve your attitude, shift your perspective, broaden your horizon, sharpen your decisions, and help you more carefully measure your words. And all of this is yours to be had in exchange for making the simple choice to listen for God. Truly, I don't know anyone prioritizing the voice of the Lord who isn't hearing his voice.

And yet despite the lavish benefits inherent in this largely one-sided exchange between God and us, something deep inside us struggles to give him a yes. We've heard the stories about God. We've memorized John 3:16. We get that his whole deal is about forgiveness of sin through the bloody cross of Christ. The puzzle pieces start to come together in our minds, causing us to strongly suspect that if we let God start nosing around in our daily dealings—in our *conversations*, no less—he will expect us to be forgiving too. In response to these suspicions, we fold our arms across our chests and in the huffy tone of a preschooler say, "But I don't *want* to forgive." (Not surprisingly, the Enemy doesn't want us to forgive, either.)

It's a tough position to hold, because life is chock-full of relationships with people, and those relationships are anything but clean and simple. We're messy through and through, and that messiness is what causes us to sin. We sin by saying the wrong thing at the wrong time or by not saying the right thing at the right time or by saying nothing at all when we ought to speak up or by doing a verbal vomit when we'd be better off zipping our lips.

Inevitably these conversational missteps wind up hurting those we're talking to, and unless forgiveness unfolds between us and them, the Enemy wins by causing division. Based on concepts we've already discussed, we know that's never a productive thing: division leads to isolation, isolation leads to destruction, and destruction is the opposite of God's plan.

To arrest this downward spiral, God says, *Take the high road, please. I can use messy people to help you clean up your messes. I can do some beautiful work here, if you'll let me in. The tension I'm asking you to work through in your relationships paves the path toward spiritual maturity. If you isolate, you'll wind up immature and weird, but if you'll engage, iron will sharpen iron, and good things will come.*

God stops partway through his explanation, halted by the sight of us still standing there with arms folded, obstinacy written all over our faces. As it turns out, we desperately want forgiveness for ourselves, even as we selfishly withhold it from everyone else.

"YOU FIRST"

Jesus told a story in Matthew 18 that is emblematic of this exact theme. So you won't glaze over at the sight of a familiar Bible story, I'm going to make the unilateral decision to invite you into the story as the main character. (Are you feeling good about this?)

According to the text, the first thing we learn about you is that you're in debt. As in you've maxed out every credit card, you've drawn on every line of credit the bank extends, and you've exhausted your boss's willingness to advance your pay month after month.

To make matters worse, you tried to alleviate your financial woes by giving online Fantasy Football betting a try. You're an avid NFL fan and figured if anyone could net a win, it was you. And so you went all in with the remaining dribs and drabs of savings you had in your account, fingers crossed that everything would work out in the end.

A few days later you receive an email informing you that the betting service is having trouble collecting the amount due because of "insufficient funds." Your heart sinks into your gut as you scroll down to find the total being sought: $1.2 million. *What have I done?* you think. Your mind races to find an escape hatch somewhere, somehow. But you know that search is in vain. There is no escape.

In reflecting on your life, you start tabulating all you'll lose: your house, your car, your dignity, your future, your hope. Could you go to prison for something like this? You add loss of freedom to the list, just in case.

You decide to plead for mercy, thinking you have nothing to lose and everything to gain. You sit down at your laptop and begin to type "To whom it may concern ..."

Twenty minutes later you straighten in your chair, satisfied with your letter. You shoot a prayer toward heaven as you hit Send and then close your eyes and exhale. To your surprise, within five minutes your computer sounds the little ding telling you a new message has arrived. You open the note, read the first two lines, and feel tears springing to your eyes. "Kind sir," the message reads, "we have decided to wipe away your debt of $1.2 million. As far as our accounts are concerned, you have been categorized as *paid in full*. Have a good day."

You can hardly believe your eyes. All that money you owed, *completely wiped away*? You walk around your living room aimlessly, just trying to soak in all this means. Eventually you stop before your front window to take in the warmth of the sun. That's when you notice your neighbor there in his yard, bagging leaves. At the sight of him you remember he never paid you back the money he borrowed last year for a mortgage payment when he was down on his luck. How could you have forgotten about that? What was it—eight hundred, nine hundred bucks? Fueled with confidence from the financial win you just enjoyed, you decide to get your money back. *Yes!* the Enemy cheers. *Don't let him get away with this! Go get what's yours, right now.*

Minutes into your conversation with your neighbor about the debt he failed to repay, you can tell things are heading south. "I'm sorry, man," he says shaking his head and staring at his shoes. "I don't have it right now."

"This is unbelievable!" you hear yourself say to him. "I thought you were my friend! I'll see you in small-claims court, *buddy*. I'll sue you for the grand you owe me, and more!"

(Whew! A little harsh, don't you think? Remind me never to buy a house next to yours.)

"You choose grace over judgment for yourself," Jesus was saying in the parable, "and then turn around and dispense judgment to others instead of grace. You've got it all wrong! If grace is what you want, then grace is what you should also give. If forgiveness is what you desire, then you must choose to forgive others."

Jesus knew we won't get out of this life without a few relational battle scars to show for living. We will be betrayed. Our rights will be violated. We will be gossiped about. We will be lied about—and to. We'll get hurt. And to these realities and a thousand more he said, "If you forgive other people when they sin against you, your heavenly Father will also forgive you. But if you do not forgive others their sins, your Father will not forgive your sins" (Matt. 6:14–15).

(Ouch, Jesus! That's going to leave a mark.)

Our obstinacy shifts to outrage as we weigh the implications of this command. "Do you know what he said about me?" we protest. "Do you have any clue what she did? I did nothing to deserve this! You want me to forgive? You've got to be kidding me!"

"Release them," Jesus says, standing firm as an oak tree on his point. "I won't change my mind on this. If you want forgiveness, you must extend forgiveness. And not just once, but *all the time*."

We replay the story in our mind's eye of the apostle Peter asking Jesus how many times he needed to forgive a brother or sister who sinned against him. Thinking he was being generous, Peter proffered a guess: "Up to seven times?"

Jesus answered, "I tell you, not seven times, but seventy-seven times" (18:21–22).

We feel for Peter here, don't we? Jesus is vying for seventy-seven forgivenesses, while we can barely wrap our minds around even one.

WHAT FORGIVENESS ISN'T

Part of the challenge we face in extending forgiveness is knowing what forgiveness even is. While you may think forgiveness means simply sweeping an issue under the rug, which is what Satan certainly goads us to do, with the intention of never allowing it to reemerge, the truth is that you could superglue that rug to the floor, and the issue is still going to get out one day.

Forgiveness Does Not Mean Denial

Once you pack enough issues under that rug and they're in there nice and tight, the conditions are perfect for the whole enchilada to suddenly blow. I call this the living-stick-of-dynamite dynamic. You deny the tension with your husband that betrays a bigger problem and pack, pack, pack it under the rug. You deny the frustrations with your daughter that point to the offense you feel and pack, pack, pack more under the rug. You deny the rude comments your boss made to you last week and pack still more under there. Pack, pack, pack, pack, pack, pack, until one day, look out: *kaboom!*

In the end, the pain of ignoring an offense will eventually become more agonizing than the issue itself ever was. Forgiveness is not denial.

Forgiveness Does Not Seek Revenge

A soldier serving in Iraq received a letter from his girlfriend back home, which alerted him to the fact that, while she would always love him, she had met someone else and was now engaged to be married. She went on to say that she wanted back the picture she had mailed him months ago. She had lost the digital file and needed his copy for the engagement announcement.

Well, this soldier's platoon buddies rallied around him and hatched a plan. They gathered all the pictures they could find—of their girlfriends, sisters, and wives—and shoved them into a box. The soldier scratched out a brief letter and taped it to the box before dropping it in the mail. It read, "Jen, congratulations on your new relationship. Happy to return your photo, but you'll have to dig it out from the ones in this box, because for the life of me, I can't remember what you look like."

Ah, *sweet revenge.*

Except that it never tastes sweet for long.

Forgiveness doesn't strive for vindication, for somehow evening the score. That's what Satan wants us to do. "You hurt me? Fine! I'll hurt you back!" Nope. We can't surrender one of Jesus's commands by sabotaging another. Romans 12:19 tells us, "Do not take revenge, my dear friends, but leave room for God's wrath, for it is written: 'It is mine to avenge; I will repay,' says the Lord."

Forgiveness Does Not Equal Restored Trust

Forgiveness doesn't necessarily mean the complete restoration of trust after someone has deceived you. Listen, Jesus commands us to *forgive* each other, not to trust each other. We're told to trust God and forgive each other. The extent to which we choose to trust each other depends on a whole host of variables, some of which we can control and some of which we cannot.

A decade ago, a very close friend of mine did something that broke our friendship in two. It was a violation that cut me to the quick, and for months I wrestled with forgiving him. Even as Satan delighted in my persistent bitterness, God kept reminding me that unless I forgave, I wouldn't receive forgiveness myself. Eventually I chose to release the man to God. These days, whenever I think of my former friend, I can pray for him and bless him with a sincere heart. But, barring his earnest repentance, one thing I'll never do is allow him back into my inner circle of friends. Forgiveness doesn't involve signing up to be played for a fool. So, what does it involve? Let me move to the most straightforward definition I know.

WHAT FORGIVENESS IS

To forgive is to erase the wrong you've been done, the hurt you've endured, the debt you're owed. It's saying, "Yes, I was victimized, but I refuse to play the victim as a result. God, you restore what was stolen. You come in and set everything right."

Admittedly, praying this prayer is an act of faith, but that's the only way forgiveness works. Whenever another person's words or deeds have harmed us, the most important thing we can do is hand that plot of scorched earth back to God, trusting that the One who is all powerful will plant something fruitful there. *That's* what forgiveness is.

"Thank You. Hear Me. Help Me."

I think of the process of forgiveness as happening in three parts—gratitude, honesty, and openness to moving ahead. Let's take each one in turn.

First, I find a posture of gratitude enormously helpful on the heels of being hurt. You'll recall that Jesus included in the prayer he taught his disciples, "Forgive us our debts, as we also have forgiven our debtors" (Matt. 6:12). This idea that God has fully forgiven me works wonders in keeping me straight on just how debt ridden I was.

So whenever someone dings me, the first thing I (try to) do is come before God and say, *Father, thank you for forgiving me for all the ways I've dinged you. I'm so sorry for all the times I sinned against you and rebelled against you and broke your heart by going my own way. I'm sorry, Lord. Thank you for forgiving me for that. I receive your forgiveness afresh right now.* Then I lavish God with praise, thanking him sincerely for the gift of his forgiveness, until my attention has totally shifted from being irked with whomever wronged me to being grateful to my loving Lord.

Once that attitude adjustment is in place, I move to the second part of forgiveness, which is telling God the truth about how I feel. That night on my back deck, humbled by God's quiet admonishment—*Brady, I'd love to have a conversation with you tonight, but I can't cut through the noise*—I told him I was sorry for being so distracted and asked him to give me the grace needed to forgive the man I'd been hypothetically conversing with, the one who had done me wrong. And as much as I was able, I shifted my focus away from the conversation between the Enemy and me to the conversation at hand, the one between God and me. "What a night you've put together," I started as I took in the moon and the stars. I exhaled my frustration and pain and said, "Thanks for being here, God …"

Later that night I caught myself replaying the conversation I'd had earlier in the week with the man who hurt me. *Some friend he is!* the Enemy taunted. *You don't have to take that, Brady. Stand up for yourself!* This time I knew better than to let anger have its way. *Father,* I prayed, more quickly this time, *help me get past this feeling of being wronged. Help me keep choosing forgiveness.*

Immediately on the heels of that prayer, I sensed a prompting from God to write the man a letter. I wasn't going to mail it; I was simply going to get my thoughts out on paper so that I could name my emotions and move on. So I complied. I took out a few pieces of paper and a pen, aware that this kind of letter had no business residing on any hard drive anywhere.

I sat and filled the entire first page with graphic details of what this "friend" had done to me, the offenses he'd committed, one by one. It was agonizing to trudge back through everything that had happened—but it was also cathartic. I wrote and wrote until all of it was there on the pages in black ink, staring back at me, heated scrawls of hurt.

I flipped the sheet of paper over and began detailing the damage this man's words and actions had done. I wrote about the self-doubt he'd caused in my heart, the feelings of despondency he'd set into motion, the difficult ripple effects I'd been made to deal with because of his immaturity and pride. I was as honest and thorough in my account as I knew how to be. When I finished that part of the letter, the pain was as raw and real as ever.

But I didn't end things there. I reached for a fresh piece of paper and began logging prayer requests I wanted to pray on this man's behalf. I asked God to bless him. To deal gently with him. To heal the parts of his heart that had been broken. To bring supernatural guidance into his life. I prayed that he would choose righteousness at every opportunity, and that as a result, the future would smile on him. I prayed he would know deep peace.

I pulled a deck chair in front of me after I'd completed my letter and read the letter aloud as though he were sitting before me, face-to-face. I lodged my complaints and offered my blessings.

Then I fed the letter through my shredder, sending my bitterness with it as it went. I asked God to help me move forward, which leads me to the final step in the process.

The third part of forgiveness involves my asking God for help to release the offender and move forward into the future God has in store for me. *Give me the ability, the grace, the strength, the love, to forgive what this person has done,* I pray. *I'm a person of forgiveness because you are a forgiving God. Help me be quick to extend mercy instead of judgment. Help me not hold this offense against him (or her). By your power, help me release this person to you. Help me move forward in joy and peace.*

I have to stop and ask you: Are these concepts ringing true for you? Is someone coming to mind as you read my words? Someone you know you need to forgive? If so, let today be a day of grace. "Enter [God's] gates with thanksgiving," Psalm 100:4 says, "and his courts with praise; give thanks to him and praise his name." Tell God how grateful you are that you have been forgiven through his Son's great sacrifice. Spend a few moments meditating on how it feels to have your scarlet sins washed "white as snow" (Isa. 1:18). Tell him the truth about the wrong you've suffered, and then enlist his help in releasing the transgressor to his tender care. Forgiveness is no onetime, quick-fix event, but it comes with a promise that if we'll engage in this redemptive process, we'll emerge victorious.

I'm not just talking about relational victory—though that's definitely there—I'm saying we'll win spiritually and emotionally too. Forgiveness is for healing the *whole* heart.

VICTORY FOR THOSE WHO FORGIVE

In Luke 4, after we read of Jesus's temptations in the wilderness, we see him returning to Galilee "in the power of the Spirit" (v. 14). News about him began spreading throughout the countryside. He began appointing apostles and teaching in synagogues and ministering to people in need. He went to his hometown of Nazareth, and on the Sabbath, he spoke those famous words we looked at earlier from the book of Isaiah about who he was and why he'd come:

> The Spirit of the Lord is on me,
>> because he has anointed me
>> to proclaim good news to the poor.
> He has sent me to proclaim freedom for the
>> prisoners
> and recovery of sight for the blind,
>> to set the oppressed free,
>> to proclaim the year of the Lord's favor.
>> (vv. 18–19)

And then, with everyone's eyes "fastened on him" (v. 20), he rolled up the scroll on which that prophecy was printed and sat down. After which everyone spoke well of him, saying how "amazed" (v. 22) they were by his words.

What I want you to catch is that after Jesus made it successfully through his trials and temptations, he was able to join his heavenly Father in kingdom-oriented work. The same is true for us. As we stand firm against the schemes of Satan, choosing truth instead of fallacy, kindness instead of anger, and forgiveness instead of revenge, we free ourselves up to move ahead with what God has called us to do. Not to steal the next chapter's thunder, but that mission has a lot to do with *love*. It's tough to love people we can't find room in our hearts to forgive, after all, which is why the sequence is what it is.

When we walk around eager to extend forgiveness, we become the most loving versions of ourselves we've ever been. Why? Because we've released the burden of putting people who hurt us in their places. We've turned that burden over to God and are trusting him to take things from there. We don't have to join the Enemy in his mission to divide and destroy our lives, a mission that's destined for destruction in the end. We can go a different way. We can go unity's way instead, and I think it's critical that we do.

Benjamin Franklin famously said, "We must all hang together, or assuredly we shall all hang separately," words I believe are just as true now as they were at the signing of the Declaration of Independence. If we refuse unity's invitation, the Enemy will pick us apart. Our very survival, I believe, hinges on our willingness to love one another, care for one another, walk alongside one another, and bear each other's burdens day by day. This is how we resist Satan's evil enticements: by staying in the game and standing strong.

TUNING IN | CHAPTER 9
Respond

1. Early in this chapter I made the assertion that while we desperately want forgiveness for ourselves, we tend to withhold it from those who wrong us, which plays directly into Satan's divisive goal. How do you react to this thought? Is it true for you or not? What examples come to mind that bolster your position?

2. Which of the following explanations of what forgiveness is *not* do you most struggle to believe? Why?

- Forgiveness is not denying the wrong occurred.
- Forgiveness is not seeking revenge.
- Forgiveness does not mean instantly restoring trust.

3. When have you chosen gratitude and seen benefits in your life as a result?

4. What assumptions about God come to mind when you consider the idea that he is forever pointing you toward a lifestyle of forgiveness, no matter the situation, no matter the offense?

Reflect

Whom do you need to forgive today? Come before God in a posture of grateful humility and recount the forgiveness he has extended to you. Tell him the truth about the wrong that has been done to you, detailing the offense and how it made you feel. Listen carefully to any promptings you receive—to pick up the phone and call the person, perhaps, or else to simply write a letter you'll later shred. And then trust him to guide you into a future free from bitterness and pain. Let his healing ways have their way in you today.

Read On

Read Matthew 18. How can you apply these principles more effectively in your life?

PART FOUR

THE CONVERSATION BETWEEN YOU AND ME

10

IT SOUNDS A LOT LIKE LOVE

A person's a person, no matter how small.
—Dr. Seuss, *Horton Hears a Who*

When his disciples pressed Jesus to pinpoint the most important rules to follow, the most critical priorities in life, Jesus said,

> The first in importance is, "Listen, Israel: The Lord your God is one; so love the Lord God with all your passion and prayer and intelligence and energy." And here is the second: "Love others as well as you love yourself." There is no other commandment that ranks with these. (Mark 12:29–31 THE MESSAGE)

This is a beautiful sentiment that you most likely aspire to as much as I do. After all, who wants to be known as a selfish, hateful clod? I don't. You probably don't either. But if we *want* to be loving and yet so often say things that *aren't* loving, what happens in between?

If you're anything like me, this is what keeps laudable motivations from panning out in the manner in which I had hoped. I resolve to listen for the whispers of God and even begin leaning in to his counsel, which in turn helps me keep my self-talk tethered to truth. This then emboldens me to head into my day with a spirit of forgiveness, compassion, and grace. But then I get on the interstate to head to a nine o'clock meeting, and there's a driver in the passing lane going ten miles per hour *below* the speed limit. "I love you, neighbor!" isn't the first thing I want to shout at that person.

One time I was en route to a pastoral-counseling appointment, where ostensibly I would help one of New Life's congregants who was struggling with anger issues. Yet, had you been in the passenger seat of my truck that morning, you would have been sure I was the one in need of anger-management therapy.

"Get in the right lane!" I hollered out my driver-side window, hoping the car in front of me would move over.

Of course the woman I was yelling at didn't so much as look at me—she was probably even singing along with the radio, lost in her own world. Finally I switched to the right lane myself, determined to blow past her and get on with my life, which is when I sensed a gentle whisper from God.

Hey, Brady? he seemed to say.

I didn't respond as much as grunt.

Psst, Brady, he continued. *Look to your right.*

To my right was Pikes Peak. I knew what God was after here. He wanted the beauty of my mountainous surroundings to calm me down. I wanted no part of that. I wanted this woman to *pay*.

But God wasn't finished. *Hey, Brady?* he said again. *I put that lady in front of you, you know.*

Wait. What did you say, God?

I put that lady in front of you to help you slow down today and breathe.

That spirit of forgiveness, compassion, and grace can disappear in a jiffy, can't it? I tapped my brakes, realizing I was pressing dangerously close, and settled in for the slow ride.

My experience that morning is a microcosm of a larger, weightier truth, which is that where two or three are gathered—even if in separate vehicles—sparks are going to fly. This is *always* what happens when iron sharpens iron; the process itself is impossible apart from a series of sparks. The "sparks" might look like annoying driving decisions, or annoying verbal tics, or an annoying voting trend, or an annoying approach to parenting, or annoying lifestyle habits, or a thousand other annoying things. You won't *believe* how many annoyances you can unearth in other people once you really start to look. And yet to them all, God says, "See forgiveness through to unity. Keep accepting them without judgment until you're as one."

This is really good advice, I think you'd agree. I mean, if a good friend came to you with a list of grievances about a boss, a mother-in-law, a colleague, a neighbor, or a spouse, assuming you're a mature follower of Jesus who strives to live out the tenets in this book, you'd probably find all sorts of ways for your friend to manifest gentleness and acceptance and love.

"Maybe he was just having a rough day," you might offer. Or, "I wonder if something else is going on in her life?" Or even,

"He's really lucky to have someone as kind as you in his sphere of influence, someone who won't cast him aside for these mistakes."

When it's someone else's annoyance, we're kind, long-suffering people who are merciful through and through. But when the sparks are flying in *our* direction? All we are is long on suffering as our kindness goes MIA. I love pastoring, and I love being with people, but on more than a few occasions, I've said, *God, if it weren't for the people, this would be a fantastic job.*

This is why you and I must keep coming back to God, the foundation of all effective relationships, because when we spend time in his presence, our hearts soften toward the people he created; and when our hearts toward them start to soften, our words toward them soften too. I wish I could give you another means for loving people, but so far in my life, I've noticed that the softening process seems to show up most frequently just after sparks have flown. God places me in an uncomfortable, unsolicited situation and then invites me to change, to grow. He says, *Brady, I need you to give more than mere lip service to this mission of total unity. I need to know that you're really all in.*

In a manner that at times seems anything but loving, God keeps shaping me into a person of love.

All too often, though, we embrace division instead of love.

DIVIDED BY RACE

Recently I was talking with my friend Brandon, who is a fellow pastor at our church and shares my Louisiana roots. We were reflecting on what it was like to grow up in the South when he said, "Yeah, once I could drive, my dad always told me that if I ever got pulled over, I should put my hands in the air immediately and do whatever the police officer said to do."

Brandon's dad also warned him about driving through the "white" neighborhoods late at night. "They see a black man like you cruising around, Son, and they'll call the cops out of plain old fear."

As I listened to Brandon talk, I thought about my own childhood experiences and about how I should be a cold-blooded racist today, given the pervasive messaging that was present in the communities where I was reared. I can't prove this quantitatively, but based on empirical evidence, I would say that my hometown of Logansport, Louisiana, has always struggled with racial equality.

My mom and dad's generation was the first to experience integrated schooling, and on more than one occasion they drove by the "black" school and the "white" school of old, pointing out to me how things were an era ago. The black school was eventually converted into a public-health center once black kids and white kids were schooled in the same building, but vestiges of segregation were still rampant in our town. Extended-family members, neighbors, and friends taught me from the youngest age to love catfish, crawdads, and people who were white. Fortunately my horizons were broadened over time, and by African Americans, no less.

When Pam and I began dating, we got involved in a ministry at our church that brought diverse people together and taught them how to appreciate each other's lives. Almost every Saturday morning, she and I would head over with a dozen or so other white people to Abbey Road, a black-neighborhood street. Having zero interracial training or experience to draw upon, I was nervous about what would unfold.

What's more, it felt a little scandalous, given the biases of the community of my youth. And yet as proof that the Holy Spirit is quite capable of jumping over even the sky-high wall of hostility and fear that has separated people groups for centuries, the experience would yield sweet, sweet fruit. The division I'd been raised on was a sham.

Initially we just talked to whomever happened to be outside relaxing on their front porches, and we trusted God to open spiritual doors as he saw fit. As those relationships deepened, actual friendships formed, and in a matter of months, Pam and I were going to church with our new friends, witnessing their baptisms, and officiating their funerals.

We shared meals together and prayed together, and Pam and I listened closely as our African American friends shared the life lessons they'd learned. They were people with stories and dreams and disappointments and quirks, just like us. More foundationally still, they were people who had been created in the image of God, just like us. As I began to see them first through *that* lens instead of the lens of color, my defenses came down and my desire to engage shot straight up.

DIVIDED BY ORIENTATION

More recently, three gay men in our community invited me to meet for coffee. It wound up being the best meeting of my week. Challenging, thought provoking, enlightening—I'm grateful I said yes.

I'll admit that as we were getting settled around the small table in a downtown café, immediate tension was our common bond—not because any of us was an unkind person but because of the thick, long-standing stereotypes that exist about them (gay men), and about people like me (evangelical megachurch pastors), as well as myriad assumptions to overcome. Would they lash out at me in anger? Would I condemn them for their sinful ways? Both parties were suspicious: Where was this thing headed, anyway?

Thankfully, within minutes of taking our seats, we spanned the chasm. As we shared our stories—theirs about what it was like "coming out" to family and friends, and mine about how upsetting it is to be cast as a hater in the community—we realized that our similarities outnumbered our differences by a mile.

We talked about the pain of being bullied—something all four of us had experienced—about how mainstream followers of Jesus can do a much better job of accepting people of *all* kinds, and about how maybe the three of them could give New Life a try before drawing the conclusion that big-church people, by definition, will judge them and quickly kick them to the curb. We shook hands as our time came to a close and agreed to meet again soon.

The conversation changed me, and based on their engagement, I think it changed them. They didn't alter their stance on what the Bible means when it talks about homosexuality, and I didn't recast my definition of *marriage* as being solely between a woman and a man, as Genesis 2:24 asserts. But something perhaps more important unfolded that day, which is that each side embraced the other with open arms and open minds. My job was to love them as Jesus loves them and let the other details work themselves out from there.

We don't have to abandon our convictions to engage in substantive conversation with people who see the world differently than we do, which is exactly what I said to the handful of people who learned of my meeting afterward and challenged me with "I hope you told them they need to get right with God!"

No, no, our job is not to convict but to love; the Holy Spirit is the One who draws hearts to God. We are here to be salt, remember? We're the savory spice that enhances the flavor of the meal; we're not the meal itself. When you're asked about the truth, clearly and lovingly explain the truth, but don't go looking for a fight, especially when a life-giving conversation will yield greater results. Jesus's pattern was to be gentle with sinners and hard on the religious and self-righteous—it's best that we follow his example in the former and don't fall into the category of the latter.

DIVIDED BY GENERATION

When Abram and Callie were little, one of the house rules Pam and I instituted was "Do not sneak around." As I noted earlier, we've never had many rules in our house, but when it comes to deception—sneaking around, lying, etc.—we lay down the law. We want to raise kids who say what they mean and mean what they say, the idea being that as they learn to be forthright in the context of our family, they'll learn to be forthright with God and others.

Along these lines, one day I was lounging around in the basement, watching a basketball game and having a snack. During commercial breaks I would mute the TV for a few seconds of auditory relief, and on one of those quiet occasions, I heard an unmistakable and familiar sound. It was the muffled crinkling of a plastic wrapper, and it was coming from upstairs.

Our family has always eaten pretty healthfully, but from time to time, things wind up in the grocery bags that can only loosely be considered "food." One time one of those things was a box of Hostess Cupcakes, the black ones with the decadent cream filling inside. As far as our kids are concerned, the idea is that snacks such as these are for everyone's enjoyment, as long as an adult grants permission *before* they're enjoyed.

Abram and Callie are aware of our expectation here; in other words, *no sneaking around.*

But on this particular day, I was sure deception was at work, since Pam was out running errands and nobody had consulted me about eating a cupcake. It wasn't the cupcake itself I was concerned with—it's a *cupcake*, for crying out loud—but rather the violation of house rules.

I waited for nearly an hour before saying something to the culprit when she came downstairs. This time it was Callie, but given Abram's run-ins over the years, it could just as easily have been him.

"How was that cupcake?" I asked my daughter, her hand caught in the proverbial cookie jar.

She didn't respond to me so much as mumble—something about "Fine, I guess … okay." Her cheeks burned red, and her gaze fell to the floor. "I should have asked you first."

Not wanting to berate or shame her, I simply restated our expectations. "Honey, I love you. Your mom and I both do. We bring treats into the house *for you,* but when you sneak around and help yourself to them, you rob us of the joy of blessing you. Ask first, Callie. It lets us share in the excitement when that request is met with a yes."

I bring up this story to make a simple request: if you are the parent of a child, please be careful how you steward that soul. Do it with love and respect. Yes, I could have humiliated my daughter that afternoon, but would it really have accomplished anything? Plus, I know my daughter and how we have raised her—a word to nudge her back in the right direction was all she really needed.

For years now I've been studying the way people parent, and the parents I most respect are the ones who refuse to shame, criticize, lash out at, shout at, or nag their kids. Somewhere along the way, they learned—for some of them, the hard way—that most rebellion is caused not by awful teenagers but by awful parenting. Listen, when young people are between the ages of twelve and twenty, they're going to make some mistakes—on a few occasions, even, *colossal* ones. (Their brains are being completely rewired, after all, which explains why sometimes they surprise us with their well-thought-out insights, and other times we wonder if they could be any dumber if they were a stump!)

This is what happens when you are ball wound tight with hormones and trying to sort out this thing called life. Don't you remember being a teenager? There's more than a little confusion during that stretch of time! My counsel to us all is to slay the spirit of *"Freak out!"* and gather our wits about us. We cannot control what our teens choose to do, but we can certainly control how we speak to them.

More than at any other age, teenagers catch relationship skills rather than learn them through being taught. They experiment with different ways to get what they want and then absorb how we respond. Sometimes they remember family rules with conviction; at other times they try to skate around them the way they did when they were toddlers. Because of the stage of life they're in, we can't control that (and to a certain extent, neither can they), but by modeling how adults should act in the face of confrontation or wrongdoing, we can prepare them for their next stage of life—young adulthood, when they're pretty much beyond our control.

We can listen and weigh their arguments (even when they seem ridiculous to us); we can answer harsh words with gentle, loving ones; when they overreact, we can show them what level-headedness looks like; and when they do wrong, we can correct them and walk them through consequences as a judge would in traffic court. Hopefully they'll catch treating others that way, and it will be their pattern once they're out of our homes.

Give this a try today: resolve in your heart to speak nothing but kind, loving words to your children from now until tomorrow at this time. Stop the criticizing. Stop the nagging (forever, hopefully). Stop the incessant oversight. Simply catch your kid doing something right and notice it out loud. "Wow! You're working hard on that project," you might say. Or, "Hey, thanks for responding to me so quickly just then. That made me feel really good." Or, "I can't help but notice how happy you seem today." Or, "I really respect the way you devote yourself to [fill in the blank]. Your persistence is impressive." Or *whatever*. Find something—anything—to affirm, and then affirm it. Lighten the atmosphere of your home these next twenty-four hours and see if the tension in your relationships doesn't lessen as a result.

Now, in case you're already drafting your email to me to recite the Bible verse about not sparing the rod with our children and about how what kids today really need is discipline, let me cut you off at the pass. I'm not at all asking you to forsake your role in guiding your children toward righteous behavior and steering them toward success. I'm just suggesting that by removing the oppressive critical spirit present in way too many homes today, we'll cause our children to feel safe enough to come to us with their struggles instead of taking the manipulate, deceive, lie, or cover-up tack.

There's this great old saying, "Do to others what you would have them do to you" (Matt. 7:12). Believe it or not, that works in parenting too. Treat your kids and respond to them in ways you want them to treat and respond to you, even when they do wrong and even when you need to hold them accountable. The results are amazing!

DIVISION, DIVISION EVERYWHERE

The list of possible dividing lines certainly could go on, but I think you get the point. Whether we've drawn a line between us and Republicans, or us and Democrats, or us and pro-choice advocates, or us and pro-life groups, or us and black people, or us and white people, or us and gays, or us and straights, or us and house-church attenders, or us and megachurch attenders, or us and people who wouldn't attend church even if you paid them to come, or us and slow drivers, or us and fast drivers, or us and *anyone*, guess whose responsibility it is to take the initial step over that stripe? *Us—especially if we say we follow Christ and walk in love.*

Not long ago, Arian Foster, a running back for the Houston Texans, made a public declaration that he was an atheist, naming himself as something of an anti–Tim Tebow. Tim is a Heisman Trophy winner and a former NFL player best known for his faith in God.

"Faith isn't enough for me,"[1] Foster went on record as saying, which delighted fellow supporters of Openly Secular, a nonprofit group working to increase awareness of nonbelievers. The day that Foster's comments hit the newswires, a local reporter called to see if I'd respond. Specifically he wanted to know how football fans who happen to also be Christians would take the news.

After doing a little research, I called the reporter back and told him that I probably wasn't going to give him what he wanted, because I didn't have anything scandalous to report. "By all accounts," I said, "this is a great guy. He loves his family. He's a devoted dad. He has saved upwards of eighty percent of his forty million in NFL earnings. He isn't a party animal. And he tries to do what's right. You want to know how *I* take this news? I hope my son is a lot like Arian someday."

What I neglected to tell the reporter is that when I was in my twenties, as Arian is today, I too questioned everything. In fact, in the early part of that decade, had an Openly Secular club existed at Louisiana Tech University, where I was enrolled as a student, I probably would have joined. I might even have been their president, given my laissez-faire posture toward God back then. *Why can't we all just be good human beings and do our own thing?* I wondered, which lets you know how disillusioned I really was at the time.

I remember thinking, *If I could just mix a little of Jesus's attitude toward the poor with a little of Buddha's expertise in meditation and a little bit of secularism's sexual freedom, I'd have a delicious syncretistic salad pretty much every meal.* And through it all—through the confusion and the rebellion and the questioning and the doubts—God was gracious toward one Brady Boyd. I'll never forget that about my heavenly Father. His gentleness makes me want to reflect the same trait now. I want to be known as gentle too.

If I've learned anything during my days pastoring a large church in a small town, it's how to live in peace alongside believers, nonbelievers, evangelicals, denominationalists, secularists, Wiccans, humanists, and the rest. Reporters can keep trolling for combativeness, but they're not going to find it in me. My "position," if you want to call it that, is love. Expansiveness of heart. Others-centered curiosity. Engagement, if they'll have it. Most of all, grace.

In all honesty, I'd love to grab a cup of coffee with Arian Foster, if for no other reason than to talk football. We have a love for football in common, so that is where I'd start. If God opened doors for deeper, more meaningful conversation, then I'd definitely walk through them, but I wouldn't have expectations along those lines. Start with the common ground, I say, and see what unfolds from there. God knows what he's doing in people's lives; we just need to follow his lead.

THE DARE: A REAL-TIME CONFESSION

What lines of division have you drawn? I wonder. What segregating stripes are you living on one side of, trusting that your huddle of homogeneity will keep you safe from "them"? Is it the poor you ostracize? Or the rich? Those with addictions? The obese? Do you draw a line at educational achievement or political affiliation or nationality or how much someone flatters you?

Where are your dividing lines? What do they say about you? If I had to venture a guess, you have a few. Everyone I know has at least a few. I've certainly had dividing lines I needed to eliminate. The commitment I'm making to you today is that if you'll confess those lines of division and condemnation to Jesus, he'll take a celestial eraser to every last one.

If you're serious about letting a spirit of love and forgiveness run its full course in you—all the way to unity's end—I dare you to join me in offering a confession of repentance to God, for acceptance and toward the purposes of peace each time you're tempted to carve a line in the sand. It's a dare because I already know the risk involved in speaking words such as these. In a manner that at times seems anything but loving, God will shape you into a person of love.

Now, to the confession. Pray,

Heavenly Father, I acknowledge before you this dividing line I've drawn between this other person and me. I confess to you my critical, judgmental, self-focused spirit and ask you to forgive my warring ways. I don't want to reach out, but I know that real love would. Please erase the line I've drawn and show me how to prize unity right here, right now.

THE RESULT: DWELLING TOGETHER IN UNITY

Psalm 133 paints a compelling picture of what emerges when you and I let God erase the lines of division we've drawn and fill us with his love. First, it says, "How good and pleasant it is when God's people live together in unity!" (v. 1), and then it offers a word picture to confirm what that means:

> It is like precious oil poured on the head,
>> running down on the beard,
> running down on Aaron's beard,
>> down on the collar of his robe.
> It is as if the dew of Hermon
>> were falling on Mount Zion.
> For there the LORD bestows his blessing,
>> even life forevermore. (vv. 2–3)

Now, the Aaron mentioned was the first priest named in the Old Testament (the Hebrew testament), and the oil the psalmist referred to symbolizes the Holy Spirit. Putting it all together, then, we learn that wherever you and I—referred to as part of the "royal priesthood" in 1 Peter 2:9—achieve unity, that's where the Holy Spirit is poured out. And based on the image provided, we're not just talking *one drop* but rather a saturating, all-consuming flood. Wise counsel, divine power, godly direction, supernatural insight, sheer abundance— wherever the Holy Spirit is active, these things and more are there.

Are you always fussing and fuming and looking here and there for offense? The Holy Spirit won't dwell in that mess. I'm telling you the truth here: he won't. But if instead you're working toward love and unity day by day, in each interaction, in every conversation, with everyone you come across, then you may want to carry a towel. You're about to get drenched, my friend.

In the next chapter we'll put practical language to this goal of being united with others in our speech, but first allow me to pray the same prayer for you that Jesus prayed for us just before he was led to be crucified. He said,

> My prayer is not for [the twelve disciples] alone. I pray also for those who will believe in me through their message, that all of them may be one, Father, just as you are in me and I am in you. May they also be in us so that the world may believe that you have sent me. I have given them the glory that you gave me, that they may be one as we are one—I in them and you in me—so that they may be brought to complete unity. Then the world will know that you sent me and have loved them even as you have loved me.
>
> Father, I want those you have given me to be with me where I am, and to see my glory, the glory you have given me because you loved me before the creation of the world.
>
> Righteous Father, though the world does not know you, I know you, and they know that you have sent me. I have made you known to them, and will continue to make you known in order

that the love you have for me may be in them and

that I myself may be in them. (John 17:20–26)

You in God's love; God's love in you; and complete unity, both with those who believe and with those who *will* believe—that is my earnest prayer for you each time you open your mouth to speak.

TUNING IN | CHAPTER 10
Respond

1. Early in this chapter I wrote that "when we spend time in [God's] presence, our hearts soften toward the people he created; and when our hearts toward them start to soften, our words toward them soften too." How have you found this to be true in your own experience? Give examples.

2. What dividing lines have you drawn along the way, separating you from those who aren't like you?

3. What would "soft words," loving words, toward the ones on the other side of those dividing lines sound like? What fears or insecurities keep you from speaking them?

4. In the same way the three gay men reached out to me, leaping over their assumptions about how a megachurch pastor would behave, when has someone reached out to you instead of drawing a line of division? What resulted from the connection that was made?

Reflect

As you encounter frustrations because of other people's attitudes, words, actions, or lifestyle preferences today, pray the real-time confession to God. Refuse to draw dividing lines, choosing instead to forgive all the way through to unity. You're more at peace when you make this shift, aren't you? See if I'm right today.

Read On

Read Psalm 133 and then write out the words in your own hand. What "blessings" of unity have you seen unfold in your life thus far?

11

WEIRD-FREE PROPHECY

Correction does much, but encouragement does more.

—Johann Wolfgang von Goethe

Against the frustrating backdrop of the gunslinging days of my early twenties, when I was overtalkative and undereffective with my words, I noticed another trend unfolding in my life. Evidently I possessed the gift of prophecy. During my first days in pastoral ministry, it really started taking off. Another pastor was the first to spot it during an altar call where I was guest speaking one time. Person after person would come forward for prayer, and I would "see" things about them every time.

I could discern things about people that the natural eye couldn't detect, and then I could draw those things out in an inspiring way. I could embolden men and women I barely even knew and, with my words, show them something of God.

"Brady, I think you have the gift of, well, *prophecy*," the other pastor said to me in a tone that made it sound as if it might be the plague.

Wait a minute, I thought. *My words can be considerate and life giving and true? The syllables I speak can be thoughtful, measured, appropriate, weighty, and wise? How on earth is this possible, for a gunslinger like me?*

Generally, prophetic encounters would happen following a morning church service. As I drove home those particular afternoons, I thought about how I wished I could spend more time trafficking that life-giving path of well-spoken words instead of sticking my foot in my mouth time and again. But I'd screwed up so magnificently and for so long by then, I wondered if the gifting would stick.

PROPHECY DEFINED

The *gift of prophecy* has become a heavy-burdened phrase, even though the topic was never meant to be complex or taboo. Prophecy, simply put, is hearing God's input for another person and then opening your mouth to speak it to him or her.

Prophecy is like any of the other spiritual gifts (administration, mercy, teaching, faith), which are meant to build up the church. First Corinthians 14:12 uses this exact language, in fact: "Since you are eager for gifts of the Spirit, *try to excel in those that build up the church.*" But we learn in that same passage that we're to be especially energized about this particular gift: *"Be eager to prophesy"* (v. 39).

Remember, Paul was writing to the church at Corinth, a city known for its beauty, its independence, its competitive spirit … and its hypersexualized, pervasively deviant culture. Corinth was the Las Vegas of its day, and yet here in the midst of this ancient Sin City, a church was formed.

When Paul encouraged the believers at Corinth to pursue the gift of prophecy, he was trying to help them welcome the work of the Holy Spirit into their lives. It is as though he was saying, "You will experience the quickest, most penetrating, most life-giving growth in your church when you learn to speak divine words to one another."

This wasn't about asking the Corinthian believers to be smarter or wittier or better at enunciation or active listening. It was about allowing the Holy Spirit of God to break into their lives and produce something supernatural in and through them, something they could never conjure on their own.

So let's take it from the top. Prophecy is a gift from God that we should enthusiastically desire and that enables us to speak on his behalf. Romans 4:17 says that God "calls into being that which does not exist" (NASB). The concept here is that, as you and I commune with God, he gives us ideas about what to say to the people he loves. As we follow through on delivering the messages we receive, we become "prophets," those who propel truth forward into future days. And the way we get that done, Acts 15:32 confirms, is by working to "encourage and strengthen" people as we're able.

For more than twenty years, Pam and I have exercised this gift of prophecy, and it has radically changed the way we follow Christ. When we're with our kids or our neighbors or our friends—even perfect strangers—we try to remember to frequently ask God questions like, *What are you saying, Father? What are you after here? If you have a message, we're ready to convey it. If you are speaking, we want to hear.*

We ask him to equip us to hear his answers and then to act on what he has said—to give us a "prophetic imagination," if you will. And along the way we've noticed that to the extent we free our minds from self-absorption and self-promotion, press on through forgiveness toward the goal of complete unity with the people in our lives, and seek divine direction in conversations both meaningful and mundane, we use our words to build up instead of to tear down. That's the simplest form of prophecy, but we've seen God do great things with it time and again.

THREE USEFUL QUESTIONS

If you've never practiced prophetic communication, allow me to take you through something of a Prophecy 101 course by teaching you three powerful questions you can ask anytime, anywhere, regarding anyone you're speaking to. Let's take them one at a time.

Question 1: What Can I Say That Will Provide Strength, Courage, and Comfort?

Earlier in that 1 Corinthians 14 passage, Paul clarified the parameters for prophecy, saying that everyone who prophesies "speaks to people for their strengthening, encouraging, and comfort" (v. 3). Not only should a prophetic word be for another person's good; prophetic words, when received, should also *feel* good.

As a church we're nearing the eighth anniversary of the shooting we suffered, and every time a tragic event unfolds on the world stage—as I write this, it was a terrorist attack in Paris, France; several months ago it was a church shooting in Charleston, South Carolina—I'm taken back to the awfulness of December 9, 2007. At around three o'clock that afternoon, after the situation was finally stabilized and our team was able to assess all that had happened in our midst, I got word that a press pool had gathered and was waiting on me. I needed to head outside into the church's parking lot and address an international audience that wanted answers I didn't have to questions about an experience I couldn't believe.

My statement would air live, I was further informed, on every major outlet—CNN, Fox News, BBC, ABC, CBS, NBC, and others—and regardless of my ill preparedness, it needed to happen now.

We'd had a guest speaker that Sunday morning, Dr. Jack Hayford, who pastored the Church on the Way in Van Nuys, California, for thirty years and who serves as one of our congregation's overseers. Police officers had corralled all of us who were in the main building, where the shooting took place, into New Life's outbuilding, and I remember holing up in the corner alone for a few minutes as I tried to collect my thoughts for the press conference.

As Pastor Jack approached, I sensed his presence. He's a big guy—six foot four, at least—and he has a commanding aura about him that changes the atmospheric pressure wherever he goes. He bent down, placed his giant hands on my shoulders, and over the top of his reading glasses caught my eye. "Brady, look at me," he said. "You are not going to make a bad decision for the next ten days." He then prayed over me and walked away.

Now, listen, I didn't lapse into some sort of trance after Jack spoke those words, but I will tell you this: My mind cleared. My shoulders rose up. My pulse rate slowed. And a few minutes later, I walked outside, stood in front of a tangle of cameras and microphones, and spoke words that I trust honored God. For several days following that press conference, other leaders and I made the decisions that needed to be made. We drew up plans that needed to be drawn up, and we communicated with everyone in need of facts.

We held a congregation-wide service that Wednesday night, and my comments felt supernaturally scripted, as though God was speaking through me. While only history will be able to confirm or deny whether my decision-making record really was spotless for those ten days, I do know that as I made it through that week and a half, I felt as though I'd taken one of those NZT pills from Limitless that cures writer's block, frees stifled creativity, and gives a person wild clarity. I was walking in the gift of wisdom those days. For all of the tragedy we had experienced, it was a beautiful anointed time.

Strength, courage, comfort—in the same way Pastor Jack lifted my spirits, I'm forever watching for ways to speak strength and encouragement to the people I'm around, and I'm amazed by how often those opportunities show up. It happened again just the other day. A repairman was at my house to fix an appliance that had gone on the fritz, and after I introduced myself and led him over to show him the work needing to be done, I stood there talking silently to God while the repairman chatted about the machine.

Father, what can I say that will encourage this man? I asked God. *What words would help him find strength?*

Interrupting my thoughts, the man said, "Hey, you're the pastor at New Life, right?"

To which I responded, "Yes."

Then, "Well, I don't go there, but I'm a Christian like you …"

The more I stood there praying, the more I picked up on a theme of discouragement in this man. I watched him work for a while, and after he had fixed the problem and stood to face me, I said, "Listen, I really appreciate your coming out here today and helping me with this problem. You're gifted at what you do. God is honored by your diligence and professionalism, and he has big plans for your life that will necessitate traits like those. Keep pursuing him, okay? And once those plans unfold, come tell me about them. I'd love to cheer you on."

He hasn't taken me up on that offer yet, even as he seemed humbled that I'd extend it.

I've had thousands of conversations like that one, exchanges that poured life into other people and reminded them that God hasn't forgotten them and that he wants to supply the resources they need to thrive.

So now it's your turn to give it a try. The next time you find yourself in conversation, while the audible exchange is happening, come silently before God and ask him to show you where the other person is feeling weak or discouraged or in pain. Ask God to give you fitting words to speak over the person's situation, and then listen closely for his response. You'll never have more fun conversationally than when you are serving as a conduit for God to speak life through you to one of his beloved. It doesn't get any better than that.

Question 2: What Has God Spoken That I Can Confirm?

God speaks to us through his Word, the Scriptures. He speaks to us through our circumstances. And he speaks to us through wise counsel. Truly, one of the most gratifying experiences in life is being used by God to confirm his activity in another person's life.

For instance, I was cutting the lawn one day on my riding mower, which incidentally is often a spiritual experience for me. The thing is only seventeen horsepower, but it is titanic in its ability to connect me to God. The hum of the engine, the fresh air, the Rocky Mountain backdrop—the net positive effect of this chore every week is unparalleled in my life. Anyway, while I was mowing, the Lord spoke to me, saying that he was calling Stephanie to be a pastor at New Life.

The Stephanie he was referring to is Stephanie Henderson, a friend of mine who pastored in Louisiana for seventeen years before being forced to relocate after Hurricane Katrina hit in 2005. *It's time for her to pastor again,* the prompting went, *and I want you to talk to her about it.*

A few days later, Pam and I had dinner with Stephanie—her husband, George, was out of town and had to miss all the fun. After dinner we drove back to our house, and as I pulled into the driveway and Stephanie began to gather her things so she could get into her own car to head home, God whispered, *Don't forget what I told you.*

Right, right, God. I'm on it.

I put the car in park, looked in the rearview mirror to catch Stephanie's eyes, and said, "I want you to pray about something. I believe you're supposed to be a pastor again and that you're supposed to pastor at New Life. I want you and George to pray about that."

I would come to find out that the Lord had already been dealing with her on this subject of reentering full-time ministry; all she needed was a little nudge to let her know she was hearing heaven correctly. Today she's a member of our church's pastoral staff, and a critical one at that.

Sometimes the Holy Spirit's prompting will make perfect sense—as was the case with God's input to me about Stephanie—and sometimes it will seem obscure. Either way, if you know that it's your heavenly Father whispering, waste no time getting the message to the person God points you toward.

I have a friend who was a bellhop at one of the big hotels in Dallas, Texas, and one Monday morning, while he was manning the valet desk in the hotel parking lot, he saw a large group of people enter the hotel. As he watched, one member of the group stood out to him. He decided to ask God about him.

Lord, he prayed, *what is going on with that person?*

To which the Lord said, *Go tell him one word:* dig.

My friend was baffled. *Dig? That's it? Not even a complete sentence?*

Tell him to dig, God confirmed.

My friend thought he'd be seen as a freak if he went up to this perfect stranger and told him to dig. So he didn't tell him.

As I say, that was on Monday. Monday went by, and then Tuesday went by, and then Wednesday dawned. The group was still staying at the hotel, and my friend happened to be working that day. He saw the "dig" guy walk by, and God started in on my friend again. *Tell him to dig,* God said.

Can I at least have some confirmation? my friend pleaded, but there was none to be had.

Just tell him to dig, God repeated.

The next day, Thursday, the group was checking out. My friend saw the man standing on the curb waiting on the vehicle that was to take them to the airport, and my friend figured he had nothing to lose now that he wouldn't be seeing the man again. He approached him and said, "Listen, I know you and your friends have been in town for a pastor's conference, and I too am a follower of Jesus Christ. All week long I've been getting this prompting from God to come up to you and tell you to dig. I have no idea what that means, but I knew I would regret not obeying the Lord, so I thought I would just tell you what he told me to say."

While my friend stood there feeling awkward, tears sprang from the man's eyes. "My church in Guatemala is really growing," the man explained in broken syllables, "and we're out of space. I've got a piece of property that backs up to a mountain. We own the mountain, but we don't have any land to expand our building.

"We have two options," the man said. "We can either dig out the back of the mountain and expand our building or move to a place outside of town. Most everybody in our community walks to church, and we have a lot of elderly people in our congregation who wouldn't be able to get to church if we moved. The elders and I have been struggling to know what to do, because it's very expensive to dig. But then again, if we move, will people be able to come? It has been a difficult decision for us."

The pastor told my friend that he and all of the elders who serve with him decided to fast and pray the entire time he was in the United States in hopes that God would speak to them. He was overcome with gratitude that my friend spoke up.

God is at work throughout the earth—in your heart and in mine and in every believer's. When we pay attention to his activity and call attention to it as he leads, we cooperate with his redemptive, restorative plans. And I'll tell you, that's a lot of fun!

Question 3: Is There an Opportunity for Me to Be Generous Here?

Being generous—with our time, our money, and our words—isn't normal. You know that, right? Generosity goes against every single fleshly desire to get more stuff, protect that stuff, and assign inordinate value to that stuff, which is why I abide by the philosophy that anytime I'm prompted to be generous, it's probably a prompting from the Lord. If you're talking to someone and have a generous thought flash through your mind, go ahead and act on that thought.

If you're prompted to give a husband and wife a free night of babysitting, do it. If you're prompted to stop what you're doing and intentionally affirm someone in your midst, do it. If you're prompted to buy groceries for a friend who is laid up with the flu, do it. If you're prompted to invest an hour talking with the troubled teenager who lives next door, do it.

On the subject of being generous with words, I'm reminded that study after study on why marriages fall apart reveals that while finances, sex, and differing opinions on how to raise kids are still some of the most common reasons people get divorced, the catalyst that *always* sets those dynamics spiraling downward is a single errant word. The husband said something condescending. The wife said something sarcastic. One of them or both of them said *something*, and suddenly they're scrambling as their house of cards collapses.

Pam and I have the opportunity to go out for lunches and dinners with lots of couples, and within ten minutes of sitting down with any of them, I can tell how their marriages are doing.

On many occasions, as soon as Pam and I get back into our car to leave the restaurant, I'll turn to her and say, "I'll be seeing them in my office for counseling someday. Mark my words." Sure enough, within a few months, the husband and wife are seated across from me, desperate for me to save the marriage they've wrecked.

But the inverse situation is also true. When couples learn to be surgical with their words instead of recklessly flinging them around, a beautiful give-and-take unfolds. Case in point: Pam and I were at dinner at the home of some friends. Riaan is a pastor on our staff, and he and his wife just celebrated their second anniversary.

When we arrived, Riaan apologized for the fact that part of their home was in a state of disarray. He was redoing their basement and had to move everything to the main level to make room for the building materials. Moments later Celina chuckled and said, "I need to apologize to you too, because the beans I planned for us to have with the meal didn't quite work out as I'd hoped."

The backstory was that Celina had made her special pinto-bean recipe that morning, placed the beans in a Crock-Pot, and plugged it in, expecting the beans to cook all day while she was at work. But midmorning, Riaan needed to shut off the electricity to the house so that he could work on the basement wiring. He had no clue that he was flipping the switch not just on the power but also on his wife's beans.

Celina came home that afternoon to find cold, uncooked beans, which for some people would have set into motion all sorts of frustrated words. But not only did she restrain herself in the moment; she was also totally respectful of Riaan as she relayed the events to us. She could have talked about her moron husband who is always inconsiderate like that. Or about how she had *told* him she was making her famous beans for us, and how could he forget something she had made a point of telling him?

Celina did nothing of the sort. She laughed it off, saying, "Well, the beans may leave a little to be desired, but you should see the magic my husband has been working in our basement!"

With that kind of language characterizing the culture of their home, they're most likely in for a long and lovely marriage. When we're extravagant with the resources God has entrusted to us—our time, our money, and yes, even our words—we reflect his extravagant love to the watching world, the same love that prompted him to give his one and only Son so that "whoever believes in him shall not perish but have eternal life" (John 3:16). And that is some kind of love.

WE ALL NEED COURAGE AND STRENGTH

I don't know if you've picked up on this, but people's levels of stress, fear, and cynicism have reached an all-time high. Everybody's on edge these days. Do you see this trend in your sphere of influence too? People are stressed out at work. They're freaked out by terrorism. They feel as if family time is an endangered species. They're annoyed with the government. They are fed up with traffic. They're too busy to use their vacation days. They have no money left days before the end of each month. In many ways, this thick tension we all feel is totally justified. All indications are that the grand finale of this earth's existence is unfolding before our eyes.

Yet in response to that eventuality, Scripture says not to sulk or worry but instead to gather our wits about us and stand strong. Luke 21:25–28 says,

> It will seem like all hell has broken loose—sun, moon, stars, earth, sea, in an uproar and everyone all over the world in a panic, the wind knocked out of them by the threat of doom, the powers-that-be quaking.
>
> And then—then!—they'll see the Son of Man welcomed in grand style—a glorious welcome! When all this starts to happen, up on your feet. Stand tall with your heads high. Help is on the way! (THE MESSAGE)

The return we're all awaiting involves the coronation of our King and the entrance of his marvelous kingdom in full. As we anticipate that arrival, we can foreshadow its grandeur in the words we choose to speak.

"Be strengthened," we can say.

"Be encouraged."

"God is speaking."

"He is near."

Do you want your relationship with your spouse to improve? Then stop criticizing and start prophesying. Do you want your relationship with your kids to improve? Then stop nagging and start prophesying. Your relationships with your boss, your neighbors, your friends, your extended family, and every single person you come across in daily life can *all* improve if you'll choose to steward your syllables more wisely today than you did yesterday. You don't have to be weird. You don't have to be anyone other than who you already are. You simply have to raise your awareness of God's activity in those people's lives and then ask him to let you be a divinely scripted messenger as you walk through each day.

TUNING IN | CHAPTER 11
Respond

1. How does this chapter's definition of *prophecy* mesh with yours?

2. Which of these three prophetic questions intrigues you most? Why?

- What can I say that will provide strength, courage, and comfort?
- What has God spoken that I can confirm?
- Is there an opportunity for me to be generous here?

3. Which of your key relationships is most in need of prophetic conversation?

Reflect

Using one or more of the prophetic questions, take time to brainstorm ways you can engage in the key relationship you mentioned in the previous question. For instance, if the relationship you cited is the one between you and your spouse, then (focusing on the first question) consider all the ways you could provide strength, courage, and comfort to him or her today. Write the words down, get them on your mind and in your heart, and then ask God for the opportunity to speak them to your spouse soon.

Read On

Meditate on the words of Hebrews 10:24–25. How can you spur someone else on today?

12

BEING KNOWN FOR
WEIGHTY WORDS

Speak clearly, if you speak at all;
carve every word before you let it fall.
—Oliver Wendell Holmes Sr., "Urania: A Rhymed Lesson"

I hadn't seen this young leader in nearly a year, and the difference those twelve months had made was pronounced. In times past I could see in him obvious talent and the potential for significant influence, but he always seemed hamstrung by his mouth. He lacked discipline in his speech, he overplayed the sarcasm card, and from interaction to interaction, people were never entirely sure what they were going to get.

I was in town to hear him speak, and mere minutes into his paced, measured, sober-minded delivery, I thought, *Good for him. He's finally tamed his tongue.* I scanned the sections of people seated around me and noticed that most everyone was leaning in, listening intently, tracking with him each step of the way. Given what was unfolding before us, I couldn't help but lean in too.

Now we can imagine this type of effectiveness being true of Jesus, the One who couldn't misspeak if he'd tried, but for a mere mortal to harness his words so well—especially one who was such a communications clod the previous year—this was impressive. He would tell me later that he had set his mind on the task of being wiser with his words, an effort that as far as I could tell had really paid off.

On the trip home after that experience, I sent my young friend a text to tell him how proud I was of him. It's not easy to move from adolescence to maturity in *any* facet of life, and as I took in his wisdom and winsomeness that morning, I knew he'd really put in the work. Because of his diligence and purposefulness, he was setting himself up for solid, drama-free relationships, kingdom-oriented impact on par with nothing he'd seen before, and a legacy that honored God. I found myself coveting the same results.

OUR WORDS ARE FRUIT WE WILL EAT

The process of writing this book has elevated a priority in my life to the top of the list: to speak words that will still taste sweet to me years and decades from now. We always eat our words someday, don't we? "The tongue has the power of life and death," Proverbs 18:21 says, "and those who love it will eat its fruit." I want the words I eat to be sweet. I want to speak words that breathe life into weary souls, that inspire stagnant hearts, that lift downcast chins, that brighten dulled eyes, and that bring hope to disheartened souls.

I want there to be a weightiness to the words I say, not of my own doing, but because of their likeness to how Jesus would speak.

I've detailed what my *weightiness* definition entails, and I'll share it with you next, but before we get to my list, I wonder what weightiness would look like for you. What do you want your legacy to be as it relates to how well you've tamed your tongue?

Are you satisfied to be the jokester forever? Or the insufferable one-upper in the crowd? The chatty Cathy (or Calvin) who loves to hear herself (or himself) talk? The repeater, the complainer, the superficial small talker, the sarcastic cynic, or the terminally distracted one?

Maybe you're a gunslinger as I was? I, for one, am ready to lay down my guns (*so much* fruitless speech) and pick up a new moniker: a kind, timely, wise user of words. That's what I want to be known and remembered for, speaking words that are *kind*, *timely*, and *wise*.

I Want to Be Known for Kind Words

It was a simple nursery rhyme from the late 1800s that was meant to teach kids to respond calmly whenever someone tauntingly called them names. "Sticks and stones may break my bones," it goes, "but words will never hurt me." What a wonderful half truth! Sticks and stones can, in fact, break our bones, but words? They can do even more damage, and it tends to go much deeper.

With every interaction, I have an opportunity to manifest thoughtful compassion in the words I speak. Based on the number of wounds I've suffered at the hands of meanness, the kindness thing is a pretty big priority for me. You might choose a different adjective you'd wish to be known by—fearless, hilarious, tough—but I'll stick with kind. I'd rather be known as that.

I Want to Be Known for Timely Words

I also want to be known for speaking *timely* words, a concept
extolled in Proverbs 15:23: "A person finds joy in giving an apt
reply—and how good is a timely word!" Proverbs 25:11 echoes the
thought. "The right word at the right time is like a custom-made
piece of jewelry," it says, "and a wise friend's timely reprimand is
like a gold ring slipped on your finger" (THE MESSAGE).

This is why practicing prophetic conversation is so important
to me, and why I make it a goal as often as I can to ask these three
questions:

- What can I say that will provide strength, courage,
  and comfort?
- What has God spoken that I can confirm?
- Is there an opportunity for me to be generous here?

Because when God is telling me to say something, that something will be timely, guaranteed.

I Want to Be Known for Wise Words

The third part of the new moniker I hope to adopt is to be known for
speaking *wise* words. Now I've been after this objective long enough
to realize that there is a simple progression I can follow. It goes like
this: If I listen to wise words, my heart will be filled with wisdom.
And you remember what flows from a heart of wisdom, right? Wise,
wise, wise, wise words. Let's look at those two stages in turn.

Listen to wise words. According to Proverbs 13:20, wisdom
is found among the wise. "Walk with the wise and become wise,"

it says, "for a companion of fools suffers harm." What this means is that to the extent that you and I surround ourselves with friends who are teachable, who are loving, who desire discipline, and who are committed to spiritual growth, we'll become those things. This is what Jesus modeled for us in the one and only scene in the Bible from his childhood.

We have all the details about Jesus's birth and vivid snapshots of his three-year ministry as an adult, but between those two periods of his life, precious little is known. That is, apart from one key scene we're given—a scene that might just tell us everything we need to know.

Jesus's parents had an annual tradition of heading to Jerusalem for the Passover, so it was to be expected that after the festival wound down the year that Jesus was twelve years old, the boy's family would make the trek from Jerusalem back home. What wasn't expected was that Jesus wouldn't be with them.

In those days traveling wasn't as straightforward as grabbing an Uber car to the airport and hopping a flight to wherever you felt like going. Most of the travel was on foot, and it could take multiple days to arrive at your destination. The jaunt from Jesus's hometown of Nazareth to the city of Jerusalem, for instance, probably took his family five days, and to have sufficient food to eat and protection from those who might do them harm along the way, they traveled in large groups. As Jesus's parents made their way back home, they assumed Jesus was nearby, wandering home with another part of the group. "Thinking he was in their company," Luke 2:44 says, "they traveled on for a day."

At some point Mary went looking for her boy, calling his name as she darted in and out of the crush of people traveling together: "Jesus? Jesus? Where are you, Son?" But he was nowhere to be found. For three days this went on, their frantic search for a child who simply refused to be found.

The company finally turned around and headed back for Jerusalem, thinking that maybe Jesus had missed the cue that it was time to depart, a decision that would prove fruitful, given that's exactly where Jesus was. When Mary and Joseph finally found their son, he was "sitting among the teachers, listening to them and asking them questions" (v. 46).

Now, two quick thoughts come to mind. First, I see an awful lot of young people in my line of work who could really benefit from this example. Sometimes I have a breakfast or lunch meeting with a group of teenagers from our church, and nine times out of ten, they have no idea how to carry on a conversation with me. I'm three decades older and, hopefully at least, a little wiser, and still they either fill our time with meaningless chatter, or else they glaze over in paralyzed fear. If I'm feeling generous, I'll take the lead and say, "Okay, here's a good question you could ask me right now—"

We need to teach our kids how to ask good questions of those who are wise! But then, just as important, we must seek out wisdom ourselves.

As I mentioned previously, years ago I made the choice to surround myself with wise men who had a little more life on them than I did, and still today, some two decades later, apart from Pam, my closest friends are all older than I am by ten years or more. It's an approach that has served me well in countless ways. These guys have walked through more experiences, they have stood on more mountaintops, they have trudged through more dark valleys, they have had their faith expanded on more occasions, they have lived through more seasons of doubt, and their willingness to steward the lessons they've learned has sharpened me and saved me from what I'm sure is incalculable and debilitating pain.

Once my relationship with these men deepened and was trustworthy, I started making a habit of explicitly asking for their guidance. I'd invite them one at a time to get a cup of coffee or go for a walk, and then I'd say, "Is there anything I'm doing that is frustrating to you—my mannerisms, my leadership, the way I engage in conversation, anything? If there is, I really want to know about it. It's the only way I can grow."

The conversations that unfolded in response to that one simple question have been life altering. In fact, I would venture to guess that at least 95 percent of every wise decision I make, every wise step I take, and every wise word I speak can be traced back to their wisdom in assessing my progress and their candor in telling me what they've seen. The time they've invested in me by engaging in unhurried, meaningful conversations, the prayers they've prayed for me over the years, the useful resources they've pointed me toward—these have been invaluable investments, teaching me how to more faithfully follow Christ.

Proverbs 15:31–32 says, "Whoever heeds life-giving correction will be at home among the wise. Those who disregard discipline despise themselves, but the one who heeds correction gains understanding." I can't say that being corrected has ever been especially fun for me, but I can vouch for the benefit espoused here. Being corrected over and over again by really wise mentors has definitely helped me increase my understanding about myself, about God, and about how to act more like Jesus.

This brings me to a point that runs the risk of offending, even though I think it's an important one to make. If as you survey the landscape of your relational life, you see a scarcity of wisdom, I want to give you permission today to ditch your foolish friends. You read that correctly: *get rid of your foolish friends.* You can continue to care about them. You can continue to pray for them. You can even give them wise counsel if and when they ask for it. But in terms of including them in your inner circle of trusted advisers and companions? Steer clear. Run away. You'll become whatever you draw near to. *Don't draw near to fools.*

Jesus made a habit of being influenced only by those who were wise, and as a result, he "grew in wisdom and stature, and in favor with God and man" (Luke 2:52). Isn't this what you and I both want? Wouldn't we rather bring healing instead of causing mayhem with our words (see Prov. 12:18)? Nobody wants to be voted Most Foolish.

I can't conceive of a situation where somebody wakes up in the morning and says, "You know, I've had some foolish days before, but today I'm going to set a new record!" I don't know a single soul who puts World Class Fool on his or her Twitter profile. We want to be known as wise, and the good news is that, depending on whom we surround ourselves with, wisdom can be ours. Foolishness in, foolishness out, but equally true is *wisdom in, wisdom out.* Isn't that encouraging news? I know it is to me.

Let your heart be filled with wisdom. Now, here is the second step I alluded to earlier. When you and I associate with wise people, our hearts will be filled with wisdom. Our desires will change, our thoughts will change, and even our words will change. As Proverbs 16:23 says, "The hearts of the wise make their mouths prudent, and their lips promote instruction."

If I had to sum up the transformation I noted in the young leader I hadn't seen in twelve months, it was exactly this: his lips were promoting instruction. He now speaks words of useful insight, of hard-won wisdom, of gentleness and grace. And the truth is, you and I can both improve in this way too. We can leave behind our childish ways and speak mature, God-honoring words.

FRESH FRUIT EVERY TIME

I've been ruminating on a passage from Matthew 12 these last few days, most likely because I've got the topic of *words* on the brain. Jesus said to his followers,

> A good man brings good things out of the good stored up in him, and an evil man brings evil things out of the evil stored up in him. But I tell you that everyone will have to give account on the day of judgment for every empty word they have spoken. For by your words you will be acquitted, and by your words you will be condemned. (vv. 35–37)

The thing I can't get out of my mind is the image of God in heaven screening the footage of my life—from every syllable ever spoken to everyone I've ever met. All I've said to Pam. To Abram. To Callie. To my staff. To my friends. To my neighbors. To the lady puttering in the fast lane. *All* of it.

But here's the encouraging part: Even five years ago, I would have thought about that scene and been horrified. I would have had heaps of guilt tumble down over me, I would have felt burdened in my spirit, and I would have resolved in my heart to do better—to become more disciplined somehow, to stop sticking my foot in my mouth, to quit being such a conversational clod. Today I see things differently. That celestial scene actually *energizes* me for the simple fact that God has promised to tend to my words if I'll tend to my relationship with him.

See, I don't have to think of affirming things to say to my wife. I don't have to strain to come up with something to say to my sometimes-quiet daughter and my sometimes-introspective son. I don't have to work to find creative ways to encourage my colleagues at the church or to engage my neighbors in meaningful conversation or to hold my tongue when someone is driving me nuts. All I have to do is stay close to Jesus, and Jesus's influence will come out through my words.

Whenever I think about that scene where God is reviewing every word I spoke in life, I picture a giant oak tree planted at the water's edge, standing firm, looking stately, and bearing awesome fruit. "You thrill to GOD's Word," the psalmist says, referring to people who live close to Christ, "you chew on Scripture day and night.

You're a tree replanted in Eden, bearing fresh fruit every month, never dropping a leaf, always in blossom" (Ps. 1:2–3 THE MESSAGE).

Fresh fruit all the time from *this* sin-stained mouth?

The ability to speak *life-giving* words for a reformed gunslinger like me?

A legacy of never having dropped a leaf? Of influence that's *always* in bloom?

I'm determined to be that big oak. And my prayer is that everyone who finds shade in kind, timely, wise, sweet-to-the-taste words will look at where I've been and where Jesus has brought me and say, "God's still amazing today."

TUNING IN | CHAPTER 12
Respond

1. What words would those who know you well use to describe your communication style?

2. Are you satisfied with that description? Why or why not?

3. If you were to honestly assess your effectiveness in communicating—with God, with yourself, and with others—do you see progress year after year, or do you suspect there has been a decline?

4. What feelings or emotions do the words of Psalm 1:2–3 stir up in you as you move closer to manifesting that which is wise?

Reflect

What do you hope your communication legacy will include? Spend a few minutes crafting your own group of words that you want to be known and remembered for—as I did with "kind, timely, and wise."

Read On

Write out the words of Psalm 1:2–3 and post the verses in a prominent place so that you can hold fast to its imagery throughout your day.

ACKNOWLEDGMENTS

Every book is birthed not from a solitary soul, but from a community committed to its message. This work took a community committed to hearing God and speaking words that heal.

I am thankful for my wife, Pam, who is my single greatest source of encouragement. You cheer for me even when the crowds are silent.

Thanks to my two teenagers, Abram and Callie. When you call me "Dad," my heart leaps.

Thanks to the great team of leaders at New Life Church. You are a joy to serve alongside.

I am very grateful for Ashley Wiersma, who helps me craft words and harness the power of language.

Most of all, I am grateful to Jesus, who calls me a son and a friend. Your words have saved me.

NOTES

CHAPTER 1: THE SPEAKING GOD

1. Helen Carroll, "Would YOU Let Your Teenage Daughter Sleep with a Boyfriend in Your Home?," DailyMail.com, June 22, 2012, www.dailymail .co.uk/femail/article-2091807/Would-YOU-let-teenage-daughter-sleep -boyfriend-home.html.

CHAPTER 2: STATIC

1. Caitlin Johnson, "Cutting through Advertising Clutter," *Sunday Morning*, CBSNews.com, September 17, 2006, www.cbsnews.com/news/cutting -through-advertising-clutter/.

CHAPTER 3: TUNED IN

1. Samuel Chadwick, *The Path of Prayer* (Fort Washington, PA: CLC Publications, 2000), chap. 3.

CHAPTER 4: WHICH VOICE WINS?

1. John Eldredge, *Walking with God* (Nashville: Thomas Nelson, 2008), 57.

2. *The Help*, directed by Tate Taylor (Universal City, CA: Dreamworks, 2011).

CHAPTER 5: INSIDIOUS INSECURITY

1. George Whitefield, *A Select Collection of Letters of the Late Reverend George Whitefield, M.A.*, 3 vols. (London, 1772), 3:59.

CHAPTER 6: TAKING GOD AT HIS WORD

1. Desperation Band, "Take Me to the River," *The Center of It All* © 2012 Integrity Music.

CHAPTER 7: DIVISION UNTO DESTRUCTION

1. Sarah Shourd, quoted in Michael Bond, "How Extreme Isolation Warps the Mind," BBC.com, May 14, 2014, www.bbc.com/future/story /20140514-how-extreme-isolation-warps-minds.

2. *Cast Away*, directed by Robert Zemeckis (Los Angeles: Twentieth Century Fox, 2000).

3. "And So It Begins," *Alone*, History Channel (June 18, 2015).

CHAPTER 10: IT SOUNDS A LOT LIKE LOVE

1. Tim Keown, "The Confession of Arian Foster," ESPN.com, www.espn .go.com/nfl/story/_/id/13369076/houston-texans-arian-foster-goes -public-not-believing-god.